D1746229

SUGARCRAFT FLOWERS
Through the Four Seasons

WINTER

Rosemary Merrills

Bramble Books

This book is dedicated to you, my students and my friends,
to thank you for your invaluable help and support during
the production of the Four Seasons series.
Without you they would never have been written.

———————— o () o ————————

All veiners and moulds used in this book have been made by Lin and David Cook
and marketed under the name of:

Diamond Paste and Mould Company
78 Battle Road, St Leonards on Sea, East Sussex TN37 7AG
Telephone: 01424 432448, Fax: 01424 421359

The engraved crystal ornaments in the
photographs were kindly loaned by:
KOTIKI
22-24 Grove Hill Road, Tunbridge Wells, Kent TN1 1RZ
Telephone: 01892 521369 Fax: 01892 511250

The wooden pots and vases are hand-crafted by Albert Hinton.

My thanks to Lilian Hinton who created the first Vanda Orchid veiner.

Published in 1996 by
Rosemary Merrills
Old Farm Lodge, Lamberhurst Quarter,
Tunbridge Wells, Kent TN3 8AR

Line drawings and poems by Rosemary Merrills

Designed and typeset by Bob Bickerton 01892 546711

Photography by Alister Thorpe Photography 0171 608 2028

Printed by Longridge Print Services
Millbrook Industrial Estate, Crowborough, East Sussex

All rights reserved. No part of this publication may be reproduced, stored in a retrieval system,
or transmitted in any form or by any means, electronic, mechanical, photocopying,
recording or otherwise, without prior written permission of
the copyright owner, Rosemary Merrills.

ISBN 9521323-3-8

British Library Cataloguing in Publication data:
A catalogue record for this book is available from the British Library,
The libraries of the Universities of Oxford and Cambridge, The National Library of Scotland,
The Library of Trinity College, Dublin and The National Library of Wales.

CONTENTS

Introduction	page 7
Glossary	8
Leaves - Basic Method	10
Twigs - Basic method	11
Bridal Gladiolus	13
Chincherinchee	17
Chinese Lanterns	21
Copper Beech Leaves	25
Cyclamen	28
Heather	32
Honesty	35
Hydrangea	39
Ivy and Insects	42
Larch Cones	45
Michaelmas Daisies	49
Mimosa	52
Mistletoe	54
Old Man's Beard	57
Spindleberries	60
Thistle	63
Vanda Orchid	66
Winter Jasmine	69
Yew	72
Flower Paste	75

IMPORTANT NOTE

The drawings in this book are not to scale.
The exact measurements are given in the notes.

FOREWORD

For many years I have admired the floral exhibition pieces produced by Rosemary. It is therefore my pleasure and privilege to write the Foreword for *The* winter book of sugar flowers.

Too often the beauty of winter can be overlooked and our imagination does not allow us to think of using the vast selection of flowers, foliage, plants and berries which can be found in this book.

Rosemary has shared with us her great love and passion for nature, as well as demonstrating her excellent skills in teaching. This book is set out in easy to follow text, the beautiful diagrams show clearly how various techniques are carried out to enable us to reproduce the delicate natural arrangements shown in the colour photographs.

The winter book is the last in the series 'The Four Seasons'. This collection produces a valuable reference for both experienced and novice sugarcraft enthusiasts.

As a teacher of sugarcraft myself I always recommend my students to look at the real flowers if possible and study how the plant is formed. We always say how difficult it is to compete with nature, however I feel sure you will agree that Rosemary has not only competed but has won.

With my best wishes.

Lesley Herbert
Senior Grand Prix d'Honneur, Hotelympia, 1992 and 1996.

INTRODUCTION

All too soon the Four Seasons have come to an end and another year has vanished.

In the winter book, I have taken a certain amount of licence in order to present a varied and interesting selection. I have journeyed into specialist areas for the cut flowers, the indoor plants and the orchid and have extended my season to borrow from late autumn and early spring.

It has been my priviledge to produce this series for you. I hope that they will continue to inspire and to give you pleasure in the creation of your flowers and in the study and enjoyment of all growing things.

Now, pull on your warm hat and gloves and come with me for a walk in the crisp, clean air of WINTER.

Rosemary Merrills
WINTER 1996

GLOSSARY

BODKIN. Polished steel needle with a ball tip, for threading ribbon. Use for thinning and cupping very fine or small petals.

CONFECTIONER'S GLAZE Used for giving leaves a shiny finish. However, if used neat, the shine will be too hard. It is therefore necessary to break down the shellac content with alcohol: To 100ml of glaze, which should be re-potted into a wide-necked jar with a tight screw lid, add up to three teaspoons of Vodka or similar high-proof spirit. (Gin is not high-proof enough). You must add one teaspoon at a time, shaking the liquid in between to prevent congealing. This is now referred to as a HALF GLAZE. (ready-mixed Half Glaze is now available from some sugarcraft suppliers).

FLOWER PARTS
- PETALS: Showy coloured parts which form the FLOWER.
- SEPALS: Usually green, but sometimes the same colour as the petals. Together they form the CALYX, which protects the flower when in bud.
- STAMENS: A number of filaments with pollen-laden heads, found in the flower centre.
- PISTIL: Small stem (the STYLE) with a tip (the STIGMA) which is receptive to pollen. Found inside the stamens.

GROTTY BITS See LEAVES AND TWIGS - BASIC METHOD. pages 10 and 11.

GUNGE A very strong 'glue' made by breaking up tiny pieces of flower paste and dissolving it in Gin or Vodka. (The alcohol prevents the mixture going off). Alternatively, use TYLOSE powder dissolved in water. Use for repairs to broken petals etc., or where extra support is needed.

HALF GLAZE See CONFECTIONER'S GLAZE

HONITON BOBBIN A short wooden tool with a pointed end for making holes and a blunt end for rolling small petals. I don't know what I'd do without this!

LEAF VEINERS These can be purchased ready-made. Those created by Diamond Mould & Paste Company are so perfect that I rarely make my own now. However, should the need arise, please refer to the instructions in the SPRING and SUMMER books. In an emergency, I sometimes use Model Magic, an American compound available in some craft shops.

PAINT BRUSHES I suggest that you buy a small selection of good brushes, as these will make your powder colouring very much easier and more effective.

- BRISTLE: Round, short head, used for brushing across the surface of twigs or stippling colour onto leaves (see Cyclamen).
- FLAT: Size $5/16$th inch wide, synthetic. Used for most powder colouring.
- ROUND: Sizes 00000 to 1 for fine line painting. Sable if possible.
  Sizes 3 to 5 for small delicate areas.   -ditto-

ROLLING PINS Do try to buy the non-stick variety if possible.

- SIZE 1: Very slim. About the thickness of size 11 knitting needles. Used for making the central vein in leaves and petals. (see Leaves - Basic Method, page 10).
- SIZE 2: Medium. About knitting needle size 3. (6.5mm).
- SIZE 3: Large. Diameter 1 inch (2.5cm)

SHADOW GREEN Powder colour used for shading the front of a leaf, especially where no other colour is used. Mix Moss green and any other green, with black until the mixture is as dark as required.

SKI STICKS A very useful way of twisting a wire to give maximum support. (see Yew berries, Acorns, Hazelnuts and Rose Hips). Also used for securing a small piece of paste for a flower centre. (see the Michaelmas Daisy).

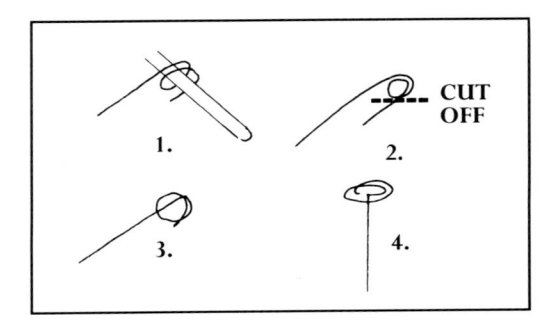

1. Twist wire around a small stick. (a cocktail stick is rather small, but the size 1 rolling pin is about right for most occasions).

2. Cut off the short end of the wire.

3. Bend the wire 'disc' down over the long wire.

4. With the long wire on top, hold the 'disc' half way down with tweezers and lift the long wire so that it is at right angles to the 'disc'.
Now you can see why it's called a SKI STICK.

STAND FOR FLOWERS Some flowers look best when allowed to stand up as though they are growing naturally rather than arranged in a spray. In order to do this, use the wires from the flowers to make a small stand. Bind all the flowers and leaves together with fine silver rose wire just below the lowest growing point. Cover wire with tape. Divide the wires into three and tape down each group to the ends. Now bend the 'legs' out to form a tripod or ring. Alternatively, set the upright arrangement in a flower holder without bending the wire legs.

TAPESTRY NEEDLE (SIZE 13) A large polished steel needle with a blunt end, used for thinning and veining small petals and for opening up a small throat in the centre of a flower.

WIRE CAGE FOR MAKING BUDS Take as many 28 gauge wires as there are petals in your flower. Join wires together with tape for a short length. 'Splay' out the wires and place a small, wired carrot-shaped cone of paste, pointed end down, into the cage. Close the wires and pull tight so that they press into the paste. Pinch out the paste which protrudes between the wires until the petals are very fine. If necessary ball the edges to thin. Remove from the cage then gently furl and curl the petals as required.

WIRES PAPER COVERED: Used for supporting most flowers and leaves.
COTTON COVERED 'SCIENTIFIC 'WIRE. On a spool. Very fine.
FINE SILVER UNCOVERED WIRE. Used for binding several stems together, or for supporting fine petals.

LEAVES - BASIC METHOD

The importance of well made leaves in sugarcraft cannot be over emphasised. They will enhance your flowers and make them appear much more realistic.

The method described here has proved to be extremely effective. It eliminates the necessity to dry the leaf over a curved shape, because the wire, inserted almost to the tip, will support the leaf and allow it to be shaped whilst the paste is still soft.

Colour flower paste green - the lighter shade of the BACK of the real leaf, or, for autumn leaves, colour paste a warm cream or bright yellow.

For green leaves use green wires and for cream or yellow leaves use white wires.

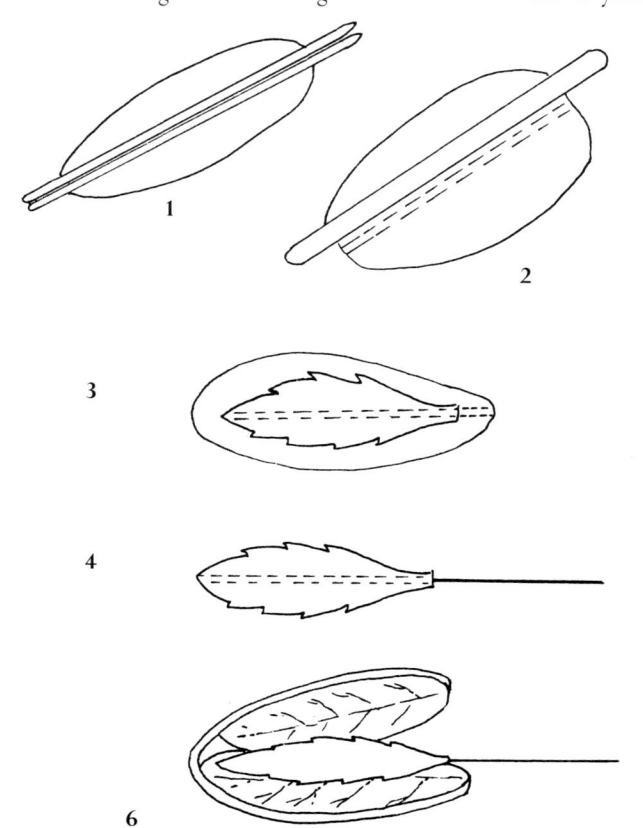

1. Roll out a small piece of paste to about $1/10$th inch (2mm) thick, and as long as the cutter to be used. Place two very small (size 1) rolling pins side by side down the length of the paste and press firmly to make a narrow vein.

2. Using the next larger rolling pin (size 2), roll away the paste on either side of the vein until very thin and wide enough to fit the cutter.
Also thin away the paste at the tip of the vein.

3. Place the cutter on the paste with the tip on the thinned away area and the vein exactly down the middle.
Cut out the leaf cleanly.

4. Holding the leaf carefully between the thumb and the forefinger, insert a fine sewing needle into the end of the vein for about $1/2$ inch (12mm). Remove needle and insert a 30 gauge wire, feeding it very slowly up into the leaf along the vein, until it reaches the tip. Press flat along the vein to hold the wire in.

5. Thin the edges of the leaf.

6. Lay the leaf on the back veiner with the middle of the leaf exactly in position down the central vein. Set the front veiner in place and press firmly with even pressure all over.

7. Brush leaf with powder colour as required, using shadow green (see glossary) to darken the front of plain leaves. Copy a real leaf or a good picture for detailed colouring. Don't forget to put colour on the back of the leaf too, especially across the raised veins.

8. Dip leaf completely into half glaze (see glossary). Drain well, then blot very lightly between two layers of tissue. (Kitchen towel may leave a pattern on the leaf).

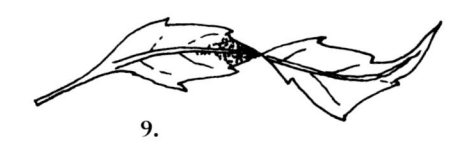

9. Stand leaf in a holder for no more than five minutes. In normal drying conditions this will be long enough for the glaze to be absorbed into the paste, so that you can handle it.
Bend the wire to the required position, then curl and 'move' the leaf.

10. Stand the leaf again until completely dry

"GROTTY BITS"

1. To give your leaves character and to make them look old, create some worm holes and 'chewed' edges.
Heat a large darning needle in a flame until red hot, then push through the paste or along the edges as required.
The carbon deposit will make the edges black.

2. The leaf may be speckled by sprinkling a few grains of shadow green powder colour on to the freshly glazed surface before blotting.

DEAD LEAVES

1. Make leaves as above but use a light brown base colour. Darken the colouring to dark brown as required.

2. After glazing, leave to dry for as short a time as possible, then crumple and curl the leaf.

3. With dark brown stem tape, cover $\frac{1}{2}$ inch (12mm) of the wire, thickening the tip.

4. Cut off at an angle, and curve the wire as shown.

TWIGS & BRANCHES-BASIC METHOD

In general, types of bark can be said to fall into two categories: rough and smooth.
Examples of both are given here, but it is necessary to make adjustments to colour and texture according to the bark being made.

ROUGH BARK

1. Using olive green or twig coloured stem tape, bind all the wires of each group of leaves, nuts or fruit together, according to the 'growth pattern' of the particular tree. Use quarter or half-width tape, allowing the tape to twist itself as you go to build up a 'knobbly' surface.

2. With a very strong, sharply pointed needle scratch and 'flick' all over the surface to roughen the bark. Concentrate on disguising any area that still looks like tape.

3. As the twigs get thicker, increase the tape to half or full-width.

4. Finish olive green tape with a bristle brush and very little dry brown paste colour brushed lightly over the rough surface, leaving the indents untouched. The results will be very lifelike.
NB: The twig coloured stem tape should not need any additional colouring.

5. To create a 'mildew' effect on old bark, brush lightly over the roughened surface with opaque white paste colour mixed with a little green.

SMOOTH BARK

1. Using brown, twig, light green or grey tape, bind all the twigs and branches as smoothly as possible, using two or three layers of tape.

2. Polish vigorously with a large needle or the back of a pair of scissor blades to disguise the overlaps of tape and to make the bark shine.

3. Small 'knobbly' areas may be made, as described above, where groups of leaves join the twigs and where twigs join the branches.

IMPORTANT NOTE

The drawings in this book are not to scale. The exact measurements are given in the notes.

BRIDAL GLADIOLUS

Have you chosen all the flowers for the wedding of the year?
Did you plan the three-tier cake and order wine and beer?
Will you remember all your vows and promise to be true?
Do you take this special man? I do, I do, I do!

The variety called Nymph, shown here, is available at the florist from late winter. This lovely bridal flower adds a striking splash of colour with its scarlet 'flame'. The furled buds are so dainty and give a very realistic touch. Other varieties may, of course, be made in any shade to suit your colour scheme.

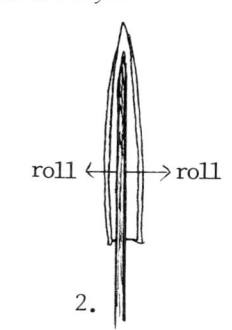

BUDS

1.

2. roll ← → roll

3.

6/7.

OPENING BUDS

1.

1.

1. Colour paste a fresh light green. Roll a very small pea-sized piece into a thin sausage, about $1/2$ inch (12mm) long and insert an unhooked half length 30 gauge light green wire. Roll the tip to a fine point then roll the base firmly so that it comes down the wire to make the finished bud no more than $3/4$ inch (2cm), with a slight 'waist' as shown. Make 3 buds for each flower stem and leave to dry.

2. SEPAL: Take another even smaller piece of green paste and roll it into a thin 'thread' about 1 inch (2.5cm) long. Lay this on a board and press a pointed cocktail stick onto the paste, along its length. Roll the cocktail stick to each side but do not roll over the edges. This will ensure that the middle is very fine but the edges remain thicker to give support.

3. Moisten the lower half of the sepal and set the smallest of the three buds inside so that the tip of the sepal is level with the tip of the bud.

4. Roll the excess paste at the base of the sepal, down, to cover the wire and to make a very slim stem. The whole bud and stem should be 2 inches (5cm) long. Pinch the tip of the sepal to emphasise the point.

5. Using quarter-width light green stem tape, add the next size bud at the point where the paste of the first stem and the second bud end. Tape down for 1 inch (2.5cm) only.

6. Make a sepal as before but use just a little more paste. Moisten and wrap around the stem and the bud together, as shown. Pinch the tip of this sepal and curl back slightly.

7. Repeat with the last bud and roll the paste as far down the wires as possible. (at least 2 inches (5cm) below the last bud). Finish the stem by taping with light green stem tape, matching the colour of the paste as closely as possible.

The above stem of 3 green buds may be used at the tip of your flower spray. alternatively, some buds may be beginning to open, showing the white petals, as follows:

1. Make a slightly fatter bud as at 1. above, but with white paste. Use a 30 gauge white wire. Using the fingers or a modelling tool, pinch out a very thin petal on both sides of the tip, retaining the sharp point in the centre. Thin the edges and curl both petals towards the front, using moisture to hold in place if necessary. 'Waist' the base of the bud as before.

OPENING BUDS (Continued)

2.

OPEN FLOWER

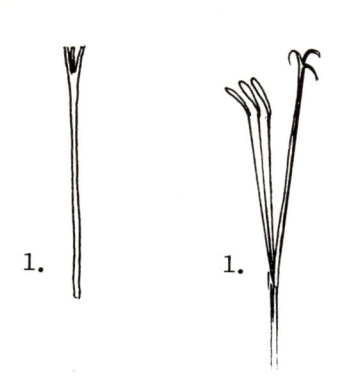

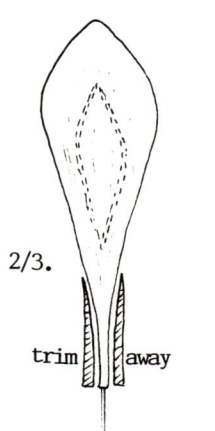

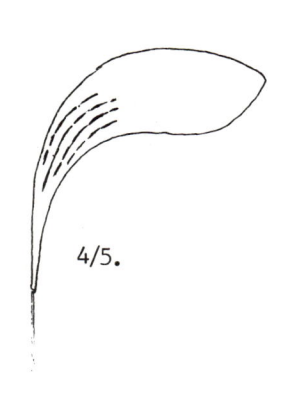

1.   1.

2/3.

trim away

4/5.

2. Make one green sepal as for the first closed bud and add one to each of the white buds with the tips level.

3. Assemble the bud spray as before, adding a second sepal as each bud is taped in, but ensure that the tip of the second sepal is lower than the first one.

1. Prepare stamen/pistil centre:
The quickest way to make the pistil is to use a long stamen cotton. Dip the tip into the water for a moment or two, then place on a board and press the tip with a tool to flatten.
Cut tip into three small sections with very fine scissors.
Curl the tips and leave to dry.
Alternatively, twist $1/3$ width white stem tape into a 'frond', leaving the tip untwisted. Cut this tip into three and twist each part separately. Curl these tips.
Use ready made white lily stamens. Tape 3 to the pistil with their tips just below the curled tips of the pistil and bend the stamen heads back a little as shown.
Alternatively, make your own stamens: Cut three 2 inch (5cm) pieces of white scientific wire. Bend the tip, dip them into the water, then into dry gum arabic powder and then into white powder colour. Shape carefully with the fingers and leave to dry.

2. Large petals:
Roll out white paste very thinly with a narrow vein up the centre. Thin paste at the tip of the vein and cut out one large petal using the Tinkertech Bridal Gladiolus cutter No. 353.
Insert a half length 30 gauge white wire almost to the tip.
Lay the petal on the firm side of a Cel pad and thin the edges firmly but do not frill them too much.
Vein the petal very lightly on a corn cob or similar veiner.
Run a ball tool around the edges again to soften the veining, which should not be too obvious.

3. Using a Jem veining tool, impress a 'flame' shape as shown, with the tip of the 'flame' about $1/2$ inch (12mm) below the tip of the petal. do not press too hard or you may expose the wire.
Trim away the paste at the lower end of the stem to make it quite slim. This petal stands upright, it is not curved.

4. Make two more large petals as above but do not impress the 'flame'.
These two petals are curved back as shown.

5. Using Fuchsia Sugartint Droplet liquid colour and a very fine brush, paint 4 or 5 very fine lines at the base of the two curved petals, not the straight one.

BRIDAL GLADIOLUS

OPEN FLOWER (Continued)

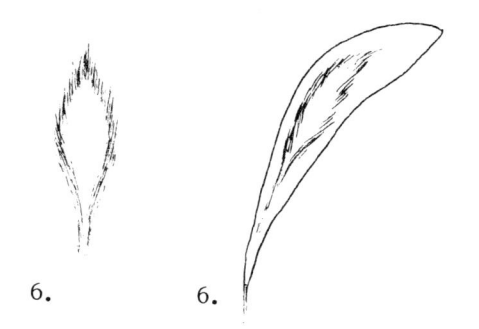

6.   6.

6. Small petals:
Make three petals using the slim cutter. No. 357
Paint the red 'flame' on each petal as soon as you have made it so that you can keep it flat on the pad for easier painting. Using Fuchsia liquid colour again, indicate the outline of the 'flame' with tiny little dots of colour.
Keep these as faint as possible, following the design given.
Begin to paint the 'flame' with the tip $^1/_2$ inch (12mm) below the tip of the petal, working in fine vertical lines, 'feathering' as delicately as possible. (it's easier than it looks!)
Immediately curve the petals back as shown, but be careful not to smudge the colour.

FLOWER ASSEMBLY

Tape the stamen/pistil centre to the large upright petal, with green stem tape. The pistil is next to the petal with the three stamens curved as shown.
Add the two large curved petals on either side and behind.

2. Tape in the three 'flame' petals in front of the stamens.

3. Sepals:
Make the green sepals as for the open bud.
One sits behind the central 'flame' petal and a longer one behind the central large petal.
Roll the paste down the stem as before.

4. Tape the open flowers to the stem of buds as shown.

CHINCHERINCHEE

The freshness of the morning on this bright and lovely day
Sparkles on the flowers chosen for my wedding spray.
Such fragrance and design created just for me
Most special is the elegant chincherin-chin-chee.

The chincherinchee has a long stem of white flowers which gradually develop from the base up to the tip. The green flower 'spike' is made up of many bracts, each concealing an unopened flower bud, some of which can just be seen. Use this flower to give length or height to your arrangement.

SMALL BUDS

1. side view

1. Shape very tiny pieces of white paste, about the size of a glass headed pin, into little cones, flat on one side, with a rounded point at the tip. (smaller than illustrated). Make 4 or 5 for each flower stem and leave to dry.

FLOWER SPIKE

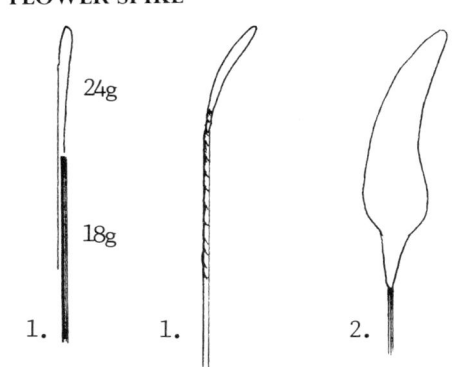

24g
18g
1. 1. 2.
3.
4/5.

1. Prepare wire: Hook 1 inch (2.5cm) at the tip of a half length light green 24 gauge wire. Using green stem tape, attach the 24 gauge wire to the tip of a full length 18 gauge wire, with the end of the hook resting on the tip of the 18 gauge wire as shown. Tape over the join and on down to the end of the 24 gauge wire. Curve the tip of the hooked 24 gauge wire slightly.

2. Roll a ball of fresh light green paste - size 8 or 9 on the Sugar Facts size guide. (15 to 17mm diameter). Shape into a one inch (2.5cm) cone. Moisten and insert the hooked 24 gauge wire, then roll the base down the 18 gauge wire as shown.

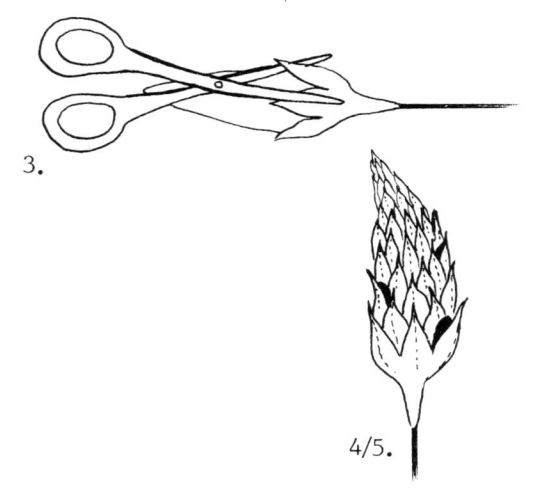

3. Using very fine scissors, begin to make 'snips' into the paste - approximately 5 around the fattest part then slightly smaller snips in between and above these. Gradually cover the whole spike with snips, making them very small towards the tip.

4. Carefully insert the tip of a honiton bobbin or small pointed tool behind one of the lower snips and impress a small hollow deep side. Moisten and slip one of the tiny white buds into this pocket with the flat side against the green cone.
Insert 4 or 5 buds at random in this way.

5. Using fine tweezers, pinch a narrow vein up the centre of each bract. Colour the veins with a touch of moss green.
Leave the flower spike to dry.

IMPORTANT NOTE: All large buds and flowers must be made on half length wires. These ultimately serve to make the thick flower stem without the need to add extra wires.

LARGE BUDS

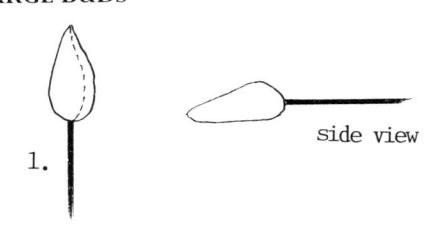

1. side view

1. Using quarter-width green stem tape, tape down a light green 30 gauge wire for $1^1/_2$ inches (4cm). Make a hook and insert into a pea-sized piece of white paste which has been shaped into a cone as for the small bud. Flatten the back of the cone and pinch a slight ridge down the front with the fingers. (not too sharp). Leave to dry. Make 4 or 5 large buds for each flower stem.

LARGE BUDS (Continued)

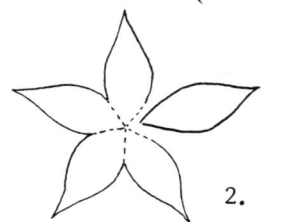

2. Roll out green paste very thinly and cut out a medium sized calyx.
Separate the sepals as shown.
Work on one sepal at a time and keep the others under cover.
Thin the edges, moisten and stick to the base of the large bud, on the ridged side.

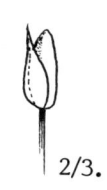

3. Pinch a vein as for the bract on the flower spike. Colour the vein on the bract as before and brush a little moss green powder colour onto the base of the white bud.

SMALL OPEN FLOWERS

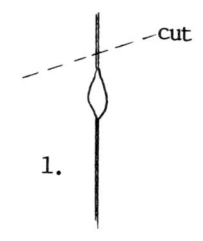

1. PREPARE STAMEN/PISTIL CENTRE:
Join quarter-width green tape $1/2$ inch (12mm) below the tip of a half length 30 gauge <u>white</u> wire.
Bind the tape to make a small fat pad as shown, for the ovary.
Tape down the wire for 1 inch (2.5cm) only. Trim the tip of the wire away to $1/8$ inch (3mm).

2. Re-join the tape at the centre of the ovary and tape in 6 tiny white stamens, about $1/4$ inch (6mm) long. they should not be longer than the pistil.
Arrange the stamens so that they sit away from the ovary in a circle.
Trim away the stamen cottons if necessary and tape down the wire again for about 1 inch (2.5cm).

3. Put a dab of gum glue on the tip of the pistil and dip it into white powder colour. Carefully dip each of the stamen tips into gum glue and then into cream or gold powder colour.
Leave to dry.

4. Roll out white paste very thinly, with a tiny 'pimple' in the centre. Cut out a small 6-petalled flower, using either a hyacinth cutter or the Orchard N5 or N6 cutters.

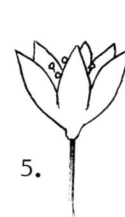

5. Thin and slightly cup the petals then pull the stamen centre through. Put only a tiny dab of moisture on the base of the ovary and squeeze the back of the flower so that it holds onto the centre firmly.
The lower half of the ovary should now be hidden by the flower centre. Brush the centre of the petals with a breath of moss green. Make 3 or 4 small flowers for each flower stem.

MEDIUM OPEN FLOWERS

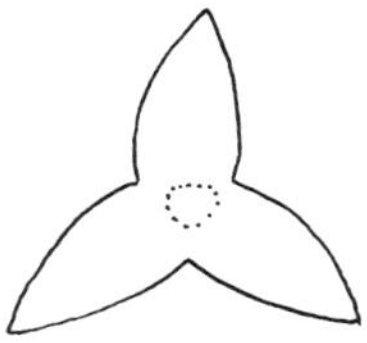

1. Prepare stamen/pistil centre as for the small open flowers.
Roll out white paste very thinly with a 'pimple' in the centre.
Cut out the flower using a large 3-petalled snowdrop cutter. (the Alison Procter Snowdrop No. S201 is ideal). Now cut out another flower but without the pimple.
Stick the two flowers together to form a 6-petalled flower.
Thin and cup all 6 petals.

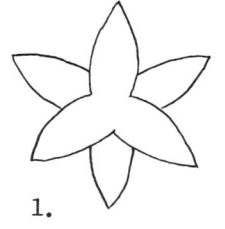

2. Pull the stamen centre through as before and colour the centre green.

NB: You may also use an Orchard 6-petal cutter No. N4.
Make 3 to 5 medium flowers for each flower stem.

CHINCHERINCHEE

LARGE OPEN FLOWERS

1. Prepare stamen/pistil centres as above.
Make the flowers using the Alison Procter chincherinchee cutter or the Orchard N3.
Make 3 to 7 flowers for each flower stem.

ASSEMBLY OF FLOWER STEM

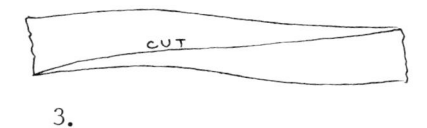

1. Tape in the large buds just below the flower spike, leaving a $\frac{1}{4}$ to $\frac{1}{2}$ inch (6 to 12mm) stem.

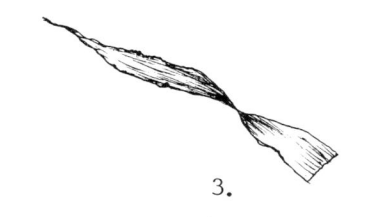

2. Tape in the small flowers followed by the medium and large flowers with slightly longer stems.

3. BRACTS:
Each bud and flower has its own sepal or bract which remains at the base of its stalk. It is not very practical to make these in sugar as they would be very vulnerable to breakage and tend to make the centre of the flower stem appear 'confused'. I have therefore shown only the two largest ones which grow at the base of the last flowers. These are usually slightly brown and crumpled.

Cut a short piece of light brown or light green stem tape and cut it in half diagonally.
Place the tape on a Cel pad and work vigorously over the surface with a JEM veining tool to vein and crumple it as much as possible.
Brush with cream powder colour with a touch of brown at the edges.
Tape the two bracts opposite each other below the last flower stem as shown.

4. Tape down the whole flower stem two or three times until it looks quite chunky.
Polish the stem with a tapestry needle to make it smooth.

CHINESE LANTERNS

The last tired leaf relaxing finds it only has to fall
And earth waits in its wisdom with a resting place for all.
Yet when the season's colours have all been chased away
There's a sudden flash of orange as the chinese lanterns sway.

Of all the winter flowers, these delightful Chinese Lanterns must surely be the most fascinating. Study them and wonder how you could possibly make them .... how to hold the edges together and still keep the shape and how to make them look light and airy. All these questions are now resolved.
Try making them and see how easy they are, relatively speaking!

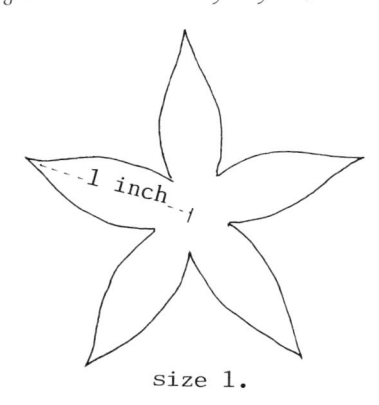

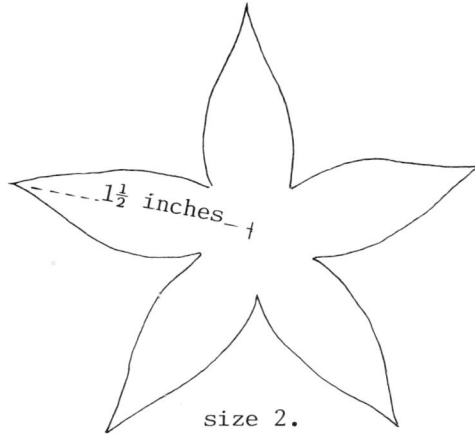

size 1.

size 2.

PREPARE STALKS AND BERRIES

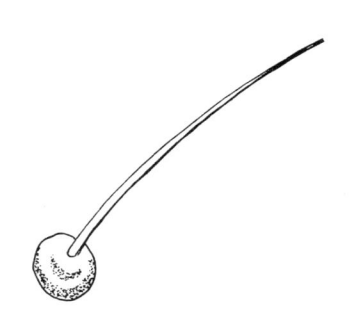

1. Tape the top $3/4$ inch (2cm) of a white 30 gauge wire with white stem tape. Overtape to 1 inch (2.5cm).
Overtape again to 2 inches (5cm), to make a stalk of graduated thickness. Make a small hook at the tip.

2. Roll a small pea-sized ball of bright orange paste and insert the hook.

3. Colour stalk with neat orange paste colour, then glaze the stalk and the berry. Make 5 or 6 orange berries for each stem of Chinese Lanterns.

4. Make 2 or 3 smaller berries on graduated wires, using a bright, fresh green paste. Brush the stalks with vine green and glaze as before.

NOTE: The orange berries and stalks are also used for the faded (cream) lanterns.

IMPORTANT NOTE: The berries must be very dry and firmly fixed to the wires before completing the lanterns. Leave to dry overnight if possible.

YOUNG GREEN LANTERNS

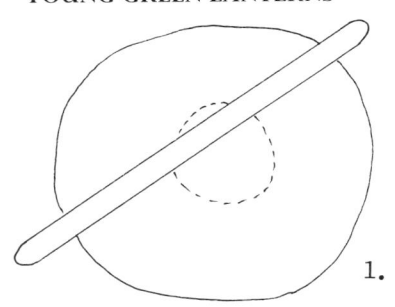

1. Using bright, fresh green paste, roll to about $1^{1}/_{2}$ inch (4cm) diameter, not too thinly.
Continue to roll all around the edges, leaving a small area of thicker paste in the centre.

2. Cut out a size 1 calyx.
Thin all the edges but DO NOT TOUCH THE TIPS.

YOUNG GREEN LANTERN (Continued)

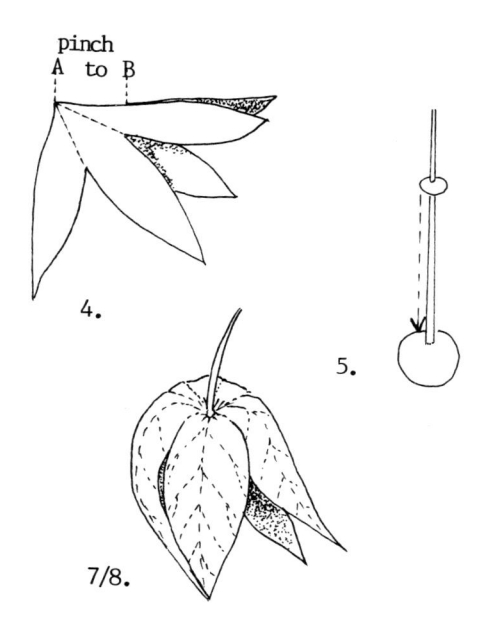

3. Vein petals on a Rosa Rugosa leaf veiner, using the BACK veiner only so that the veins are raised, not indented.
The tip of each petal is placed at the tip of the veiner.

4. As soon as possible, line up two of the petals, edge to edge and pinch at the top to make a small ridge from point A to point B.
Line up each pair of petals in turn and repeat so that there are 5 ridges radiating out from the centre.

5. Thread a very small ball of green paste onto the wire and stick it to the top of the berry.

6. Pull the wire through the centre of the lantern and stick it to the soft ball.

7. With a small pointed tool, indent a hollow into the soft paste all around the point where the wire emerges from the top of the lantern.
Allow the lantern to 'rest' on the board for a minute or two at this stage.
If the paste is just beginning to dry, the lantern is more likely to hold its shape and less likely to collapse.

8. Put just a touch of moisture on the extreme tips of the petals then stick them together carefully, one at a time.
DO NOT USE TOO MUCH MOISTURE.

NOTE: It is not necessary to stick the sides of the petals together as this can distort the shape of the lantern.
There may be some tiny gaps, but this actually makes the lantern appear lighter and very realistic if the berries can be seen inside.

9. Leave to dry thoroughly, then colour: Mix vine green powder colour with a little white fat, then brush over the dry lantern to give a soft sheen.

RIPENING LANTERN

1. Add some white paste to the green to make much paler.
Use the size 1 cutter and make the lantern as above, using another green berry.

2. When dry, brush with orange powder colour mixed with white fat over the stalk end of the lantern and touch a vine green/white fat at the tip.
Blend the two colours together where they meet.

3. For the next lantern repeat as above, using the same size cutter but roll each petal to elongate slightly before thinning and veining so that the lantern is very slightly larger.

4. Colour with more orange and less green.

FULLY RIPE LANTERN

1. Use the larger size 2 cutter and bright orange paste and an orange berry.

2. When dry, brush the whole lantern with orange/white fat.

CHINESE LANTERNS

FADING LANTERN

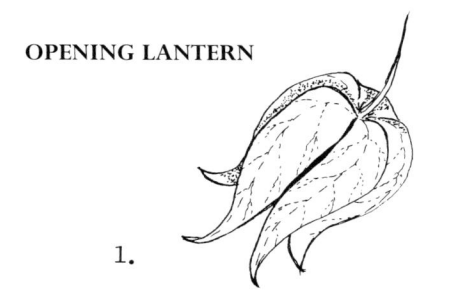

1. Add a TINY piece of orange paste to white to make light cream.
Make a size 2 lantern using an orange berry.

2. Brush the top with orange and the tip with plain white fat only.

OPENING LANTERN

1. Repeat above but leave the tip of the petals slightly open and curled back.

2. Colour the top with a touch of orange and white fat only on the rest.

1.

LEAVES

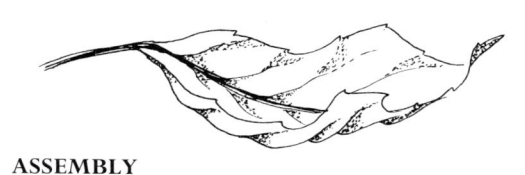

As this is meant to be a dried flower, there would not normally be any leaves, but for added interest you could make a slightly dry leaf using a plain leaf cutter and fairly simple veining, such as a large viburnum, an oak or hydrangea. Use light green paste with a blush of orange and chestnut. Add 'grotty bits' as required and crumple the leaf as shown.
Follow instructions on pages 10 and 11.

ASSEMBLY

1. Tape the tip of a full-length 24 gauge white wire with quarter-width light green tape.

2. Tape in the smallest green lantern with a short curved stem..

3. Tape down the wire for about 1 inch (2.5cm) and tape in the next ripe lantern.

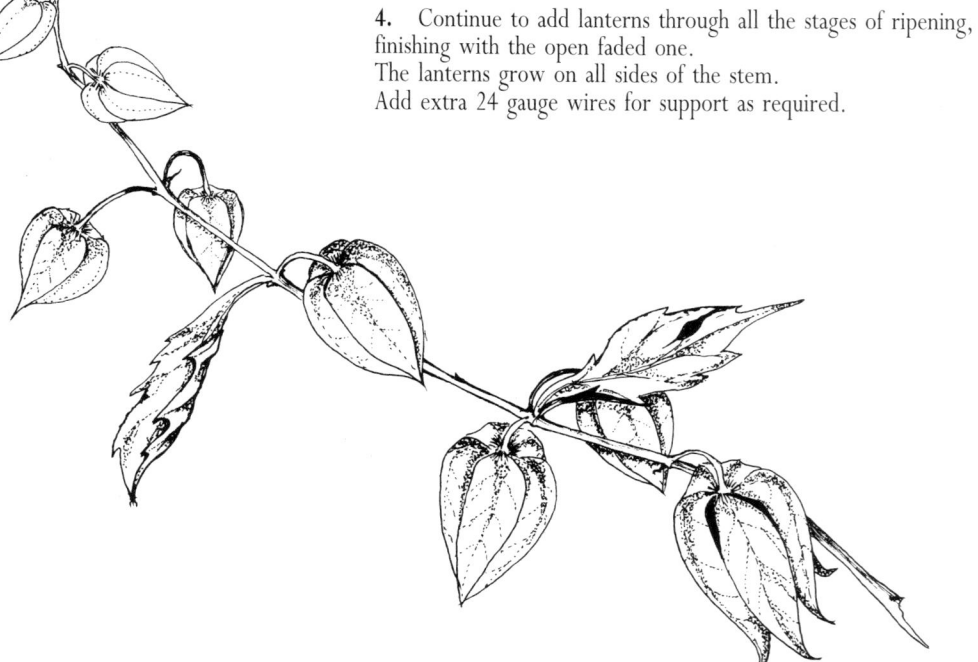

4. Continue to add lanterns through all the stages of ripening, finishing with the open faded one.
The lanterns grow on all sides of the stem.
Add extra 24 gauge wires for support as required.

COPPER BEECH LEAVES

Cold are the mornings and dark the night
When bonfires are a welcome sight.
The branches sigh as east winds blow
To make the beech leaves copper glow.

The rich colour of these lovely leaves compliments any arrangement. Use them to enhance or contrast with your chosen floral colour scheme.

BUDS

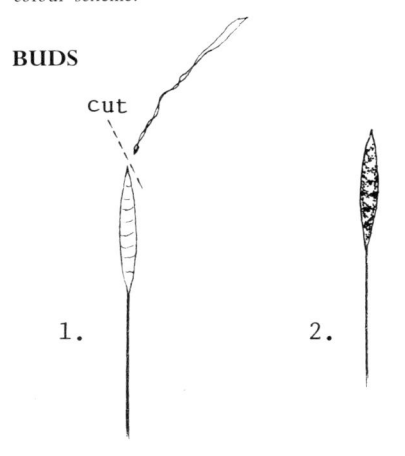

1. A slender bud forms in the autumn to replace each leaf as it falls. Tape quarter-width beige stem tape to the tip of a $3\frac{1}{2}$ inch (9cm) dark green 33 gauge wire.
Tape down for $\frac{1}{2}$ inch (12mm) only, then tape up almost to the tip and up and down several times, thickening in the middle. Finish by taking the tape beyond the tip and then twisting it tightly to itself before cutting off to a sharp point.

2. Brush the bud with neat chestnut brown paste colour, strongly at the bottom and lightly at the tip, leaving some areas of beige tape showing to look like scales.

3. Dip into confectioner's glaze and leave to dry.

4. Make several smaller buds about $\frac{1}{4}$ inch (6mm), too.

SMALL LEAVES

1. Young beech leaves have very deep straight veins, giving a 'pleated' look. Use a young hazel or alder leaf veiner if the small beech leaf is not available, as they are almost identical.

2. Colour paste deep copper, using chestnut and red paste colours. Roll out paste with a narrow ridge up the middle and cut out a small rose leaf.
Insert a dark green half-length 30 gauge wire almost to the tip.

3. Lay leaf on the firm side of a Cel pad and ball the edges strongly to thin and to flute. Vein leaf carefully. Glaze and dry with the edges well fluted and with plenty of 'movement'.

4. When fairly dry, brush the back of the leaf with shadow green to which a tiny amount of green frosted powder has been added. (don't overdo this). Brush shadow green (without the frosting) on the front edges and across the raised veins on the back.
If necessary re-shape the edges before the paste is too dry.

MEDIUM LEAVES

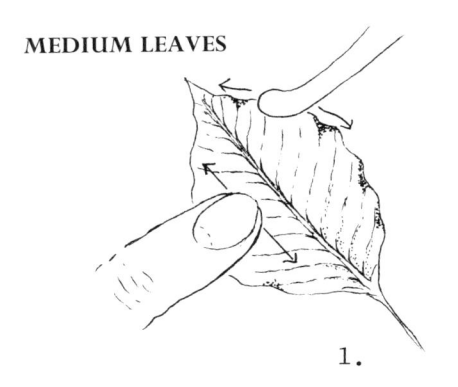

1. As the leaves grow, the veins flatten out. Make several leaves using the medium rose leaf cutter and the same veiner, but after veining, ball the edges again and press the veins out a little with a finger.

2. Colour and finish as before.

LARGE LEAVES

1. Use a large rose leaf cutter and a beech leaf veiner which has much smoother veining, though the parallel veins are still quite visible.

2. Colour and finish as before.

ASSEMBLY

1. Join quarter-width dark brown stem tape to the tip of a 26 gauge half length wire (any colour).
Attach a small bud, with no stem and tape down smoothly for $1/4$ inch (5mm).
Bend the wire very slightly to one side to form an 'elbow'.

2. Join a larger bud to this 'elbow' and tape down for $1/2$ inch (12mm).

3. Bend wire again in the opposite direction and attach another bud.

4. Tape down for 1 inch (2.5cm) and repeat.

Small twigs may be made with only two or three buds and some may be considerably longer, depending on your arrangement.

5. Brush all the taped twigs sparingly with half glaze and leave to dry.

6. Attach one bud $1/4$ inch (5mm) below each leaf and tape down for an inch (2.5cm) or so.
Some of the larger leaves may be left without a bud.

7. Begin to create the spray by taping in small leaf/bud combinations below the bud-only twigs then gradually add the medium and large leaves for the desired arrangement.

8. Use several leaf sprays together, side by side, to form a flat 'background' on which to set your flowers.

COPPER BEECH LEAVES

CYCLAMEN

Winter winds are whistling through the frozen hills
The only flowers growing are on our windowsills
So water, feed and tend them, they are so very dear,
They'll have to last until the spring
And that's not awfully near.

The garden centres can now create a permanent summer, but they still have some special seasons, one being the potted cyclamen in time for Christmas. Make a beautiful copy of your plant to last you all year through.

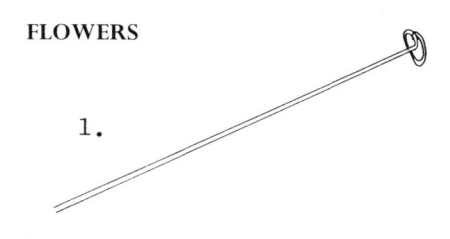

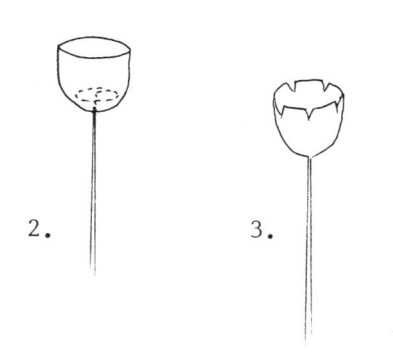

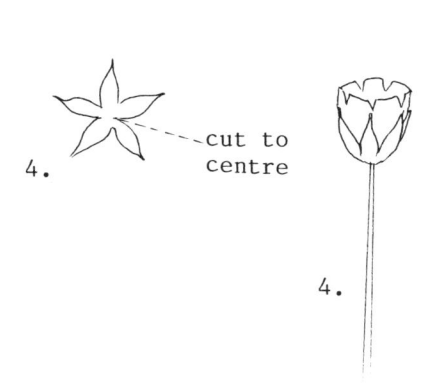

FLOWERS

1.

2.   3.

4. —cut to centre

4.

IMPORTANT: The centre and the calyx of the flower must be made and allowed to dry thoroughly before proceeding as the petals are supported by them.

1. PREPARE STEMS:
Using half-length 24 gauge white wires and half-width white tape, tape from one end for 4 inches (10cm) and break off the tape.
Overtape from the same end for 5 inches (12.5cm) and then go over the whole length of the wire.
This will give you a graduated stem.
The thinnest end is the flower end.
Make a medium-sized ski-stick on the thin end (see glossary).

2. Roll a medium pea-sized ball in your chosen flower colour. (size 5 on the Cel Facts size guide).
Slightly moisten the underside of the ski-stick and pull the stem through the ball.
Pull the ski-stick well down into the paste, at the same time pushing up the sides to form a cup.
Shape cup with a ball tool. It is important that the cup is quite deep but not too wide at the upper edge, though this will depend upon the size of the petal cutters to be used.

3. Make five evenly spaced snips into the edge and cut out a very small 'vee' at each snip.

4. CALYX:
Roll out green paste very thinly and cut out a very small calyx.
Cut into the centre between two sepals and set in place over the base of the cup.
(this will avoid tearing the delicate calyx with the thick stem).

5. Leave to dry thoroughly, overnight if possible.

6. Brush the stem and the calyx lightly with burgundy powder colour and a touch of light green on the lower part of the stem.

FLOWER (Continued)

8.

11/12.

13.

BUDS

1.

1.

2.

LEAVES

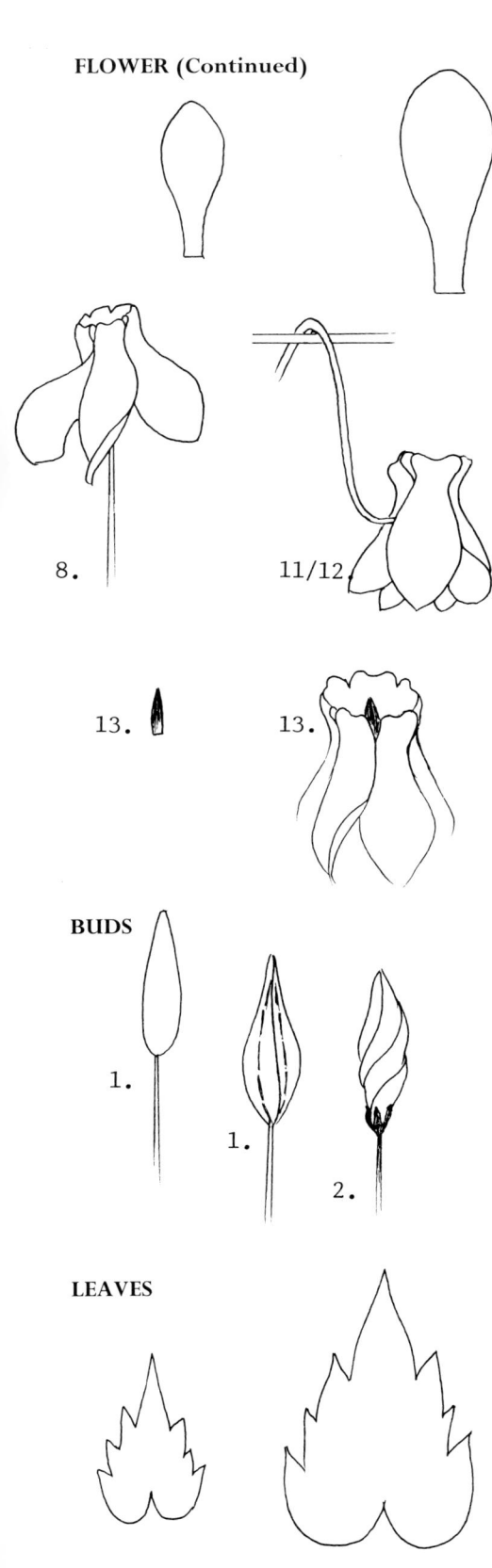

variegator patterns

7. PETALS: Use cyclamen petal cutters. Roll out coloured paste very thinly and cut out five petals. Keep under a plastic cover whilst working on one petal. Thin the edges very well, but do not thin the centres too much as they need to be a little self-supporting.
Carefully check the width across the blunt end of the petal.
This must not be wider than one of the edges between two 'vees'.
NB. The petals may be very lightly veined but this is optional.

8. Lightly moisten inside and outside one of the five edges on the cup, then carefully set one of the petals in place.
The blunt end fits over the lip of the cup, nestling neatly inside with the petal draped back towards the stem as shown.

9. Pinch the petal where it folds over the edge of the cup, to define the fold.

10. When all five petals are in place, ensure that each one is slightly twisted, with one edge under the adjacent one.

11. Leave flower to dry for ten minutes, then bend the wire down as shown. (a ball tool held inside the cup will help you to do this without touching the petals).
The stem now curves in between two petals.

12. Hook the lower end of the wire and hang it over a rail until completely dry.

13. PISTIL: Use green paste. Roll a very tiny cone and stick in the centre of the cup to represent the ovary/pistil.

14. Brush powder colour onto the petals as required, and add a touch of green inside the cup around the pistil.

1. Make stem as for the flower. Hook the thin end.
Roll a small carrot shaped cone with coloured paste. Insert hook.
Using the wire cage method (see glossary), pinch out five petals and curl them around in a spiral fashion as shown.

2. Add a very small calyx as for the open flower then brush with burgundy powder colour. Curve the stem.

3. Make some smaller buds and leave the stems more upright.
Alternative Bud: Mould a tiny piece of paste onto the hook.
Using a smaller cyclamen petal cutter, set five petals wrapped around each other so that they appear to spiral. Add calyx.

1. Following the patterns given, cut out the variegators from thin card or plastic. Colour paste mid-green, but leaves do vary so check colour with your chosen plant.

2. Tape half length 26 gauge green wire as before but leave the top 2 inches (5cm) uncovered for insertion into the leaf.

3. Make leaf following the instructions on page 10 using heart shaped cutters. The leaves need to be finely serrated. Work around the edges with a tapestry needle on the firm side of a Cel pad, 'breaking' tiny points all round. Finish with gentle pressure with a ball tool to smooth over the serrations.

LEAVES (Continued)

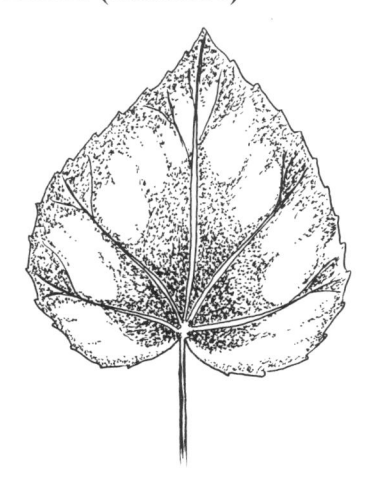

4. Vein leaf using a cyclamen or violet veiner.

5. Mix some white and moss green powder colour with a little white fat for the blotchy patterns. Or use JEM petal Crème.
Place the leaf on a piece of kitchen towel and set variegator at the base of the leaf.

6. Using a 'stubby' bristle brush (an eye colour brush is good), stipple the white/green colour all around the pattern.
Lift pattern from leaf and add a few more dabs of colour where needed. Dip leaf into half glaze, blot very carefully so that you don't smudge the pattern, and leave to dry for ten minutes.
'Move' the edges and curl back.

7. When completely dry, brush burgundy colour over the back of the leaf and on the edges - not on the front.
Make plenty of leaves in a selection of sizes.

PLANT ASSEMBLY

1. Place sugar paste in a small pot.
Set the stems of the open flowers towards the centre.

2. Place leaves well below the flower heads.

3. The buds are on much shorter stems and are in between the leaves as shown.

CYCLAMEN

HEATHER

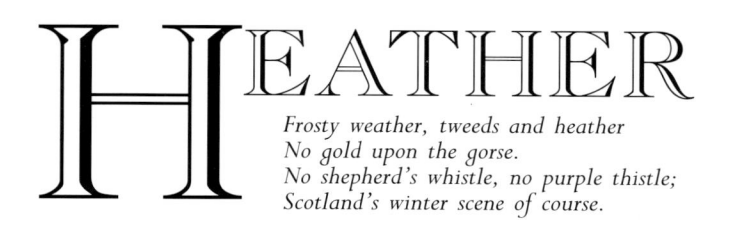

Frosty weather, tweeds and heather
No gold upon the gorse.
No shepherd's whistle, no purple thistle;
Scotland's winter scene of course.

Use pink heather mixed with thistles and some tartan ribbon to make a delightful decoration for a cake with a Scottish theme, or simply make a spray of white heather in a silver holder and wear it on your lapel .....guaranteed to bring you Good Luck!

FLOWER BUDS

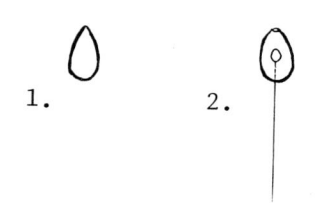

Colour paste a pretty mauvy/pink. (Sugartint Droplet Heather is perfect). Alternatively, leave paste white.

1. Roll a tiny ball of paste and elongate into a slightly pointed cone. Insert a fine sewing needle into the pointed end and out at the rounded end, trying not to change the shape.

2. Insert a small yellow or white stamen, pulling the head well down into the cone until it is hidden and fixed firmly into the soft paste. Make two or three buds for each flower stem.

OPEN FLOWERS

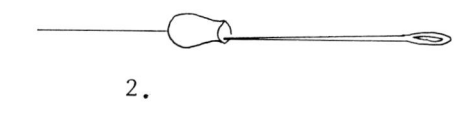

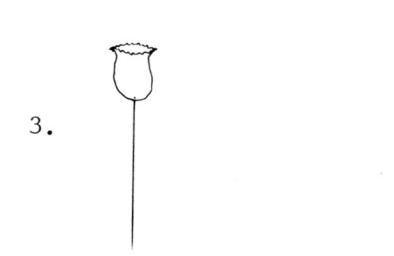

1. Take a slightly larger piece of paste and repeat steps 1. and 2. as for the flower buds.

2. Hold the flower by the stamen cotton and lay it on its side on a board or, preferably, on the firm side of a Cel pad. With the tip of a strong, pointed sewing needle, press gently inside the edge of the open cone to thin and 'break' the edges, all round. NB: the amount of pressure and the number of times you need to work around the edges will depend entirely upon the texture of your paste. It is very important to work on the extreme edge only.

3. Open out the tip of the flower as shown. Leave to dry.

4. Add a little white paste to the pink and continue to make flowers as above. Continue to lighten paste as you go until you have made at least 12 flowers and buds, shading from dark to light, for each stem.

5. Colour a short part of each stamen cotton green, using liquid colour as this will dry well so that it doesn't smudge onto the flowers when taping together.

LEAVES

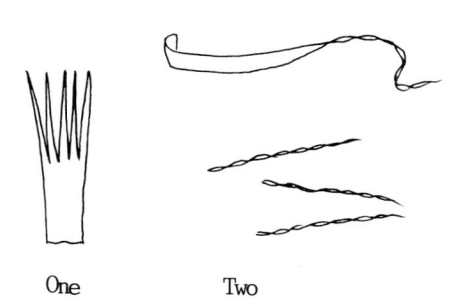

METHOD ONE
Cut one inch (2.5cm) pieces of half-width green stem tape. Snip 5 or 6 pointed strands as shown.

METHOD TWO
Using quarter-width green stem tape, twist long lengths into very fine threads.
Break off into 1 inch (2.5cm) pieces.
NB: Do not <u>cut</u> threads as this will make the tips blunt and unnatural-looking.

One Two

HEATHER

ASSEMBLY

1. Tape 5 or 6 leaves to the tip of a half-length dark green 24 gauge wire.
Add one very small closed bud, leaving only a tiny stem and tape down a few turns.
Add two or more leaves and one larger bud.
Add two leaves and a larger bud or a small flower.

2. Continue to add leaves and flowers in this way, using the darker flowers at the top and getting paler towards the bottom of the stem.

3. Finish with a group of 5 leaves below the last flower.

4. Make another stem of flowers, then join the two stems together, adding more leaves at the joint.

5. Add a bow of narrow tartan ribbon just below the last group of leaves.

1/3.

SILVER FLOWER HOLDER

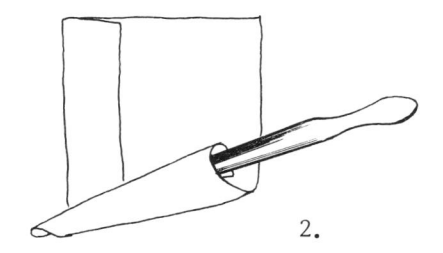

1. Cut a piece of silver kitchen foil about $2\frac{1}{2}$ x 2 inches (6 x 5cm). Fold up $\frac{1}{2}$ inch (12mm) along the long edge.

2. Sit the tip of a honiton bobbin or similar pointed tool into the fold and roll up the foil, slightly diagonally.
Squeeze the tip to make a point.
Trim holder to 2 inches (5cm).

3. Leaving the holder on the tool, 'polish' with a size 13 tapestry needle to remove any wrinkles.

4. Bend the stems of the heather and fit into the holder.

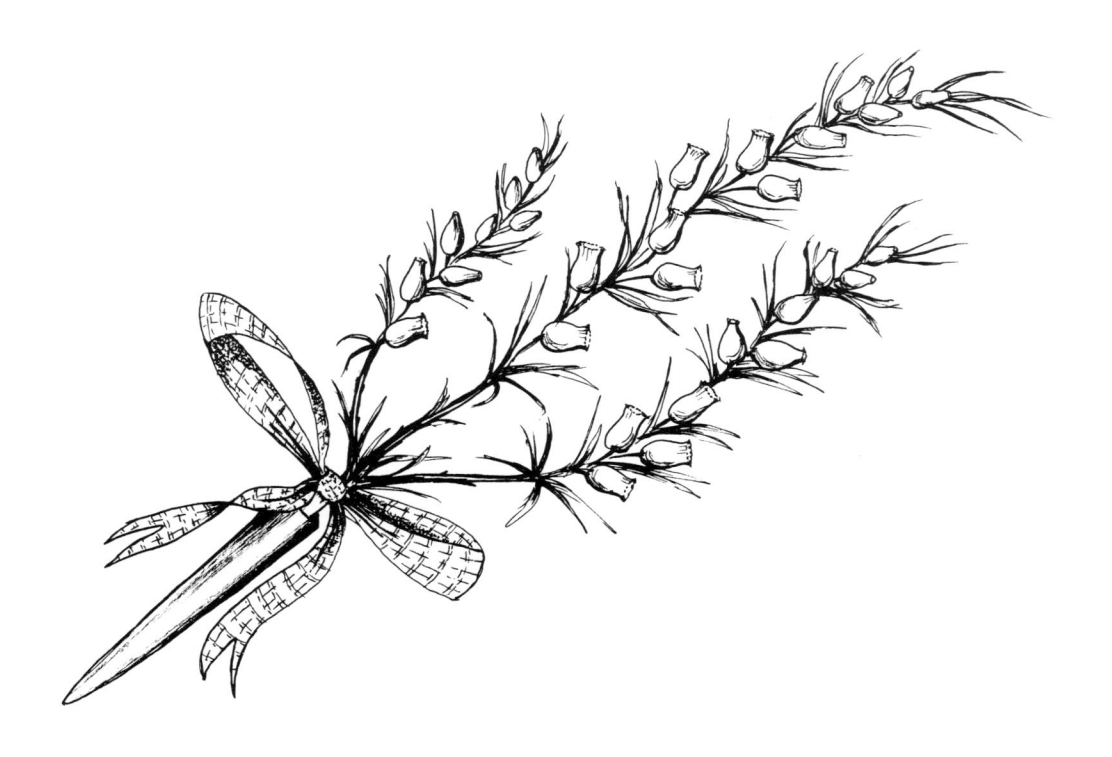

2.

HONESTY

*Gardeners plan their floral year with scented Spring and Summer
Autumn brings its fruitfulness, whilst Winter can't be glummer.
But don't forget that nature has created one exception
The glorious silver Honesty shines bright without deception.*

When these flat Honesty seed pods are ripe, the two tissue-thin outer layers can be peeled away to reveal the satin inner septum which looks like a mother-of-pearl penny. These are popular for winter floral displays and will add a delicate touch to your Christmas cake decoration.

PREPARE VEINER

1. Make a small mould for the uneven surface of the septum with FIMO or any suitable modelling agent:

Roll out a thick oval disc, 1 inch x 1½ inches (2.5 x 3.5cm).
Indent all over the disc with a small ball tool to make a 'knobbly' surface.
Alternatively, use a ready-made mould from Diamond Paste and Mould Company.

HONESTY FRAME

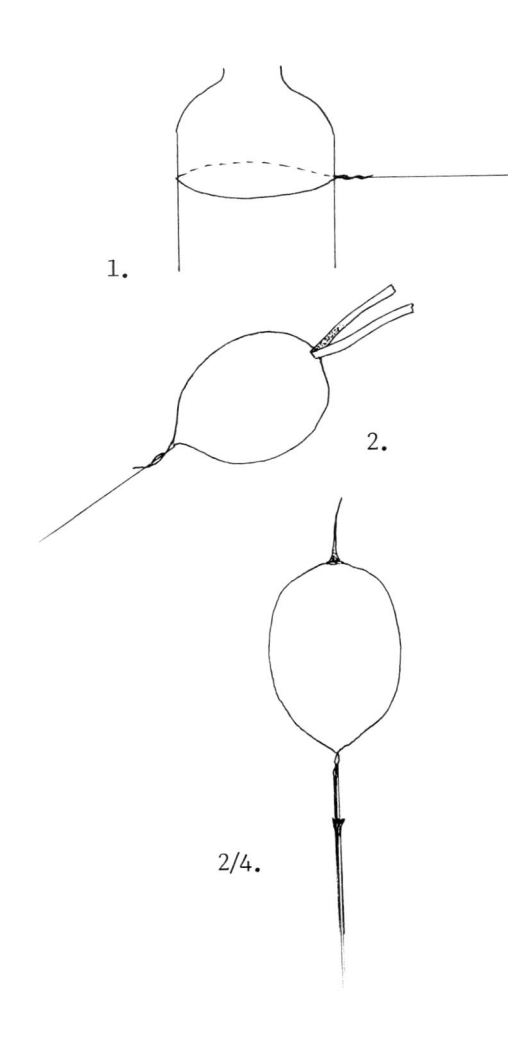

1. Wind the end of a half-length 33 gauge white wire around a small rolling pin or a liquid colour bottle.
Twist together very tightly two or three times.
Do not twist too many times or the join will become too obvious.
Snip away the short end, close to the twist.
The resulting circle of wire should be approximately the same size as the veiner or a little smaller.

2. Cut one inch (2.5cm) pieces of beige tape into ⅛ widths.
Fold one piece of the tape through the wire loop, opposite the stem and twist very tightly to make a little 'spike'.
Trim to about ¼ inch (5mm) with a fine point.

3. Using quarter-width beige stem tape, tape down the wires, starting immediately below the twist.

4. With fine pliers, pinch a tiny 'snag' on the taped wire, about ½ inch (12mm) below the frame,. This is optional, but it adds to the character of the plant.

5. Place a small amount of water into a saucer and add a tiny drop of dark brown paste colour to make a <u>very</u> weak solution.
Dip each wire into the colour and brush quickly to tint the white wires all over.
Immediately press between two layers of kitchen towel to dry.
NOTE: Do not allow the wire to remain wet for too long or the paper cover may unravel.
Leave to dry thoroughly.

6. Shape the wire frames into realistic Honesty heads as shown.

35

SEPTUM

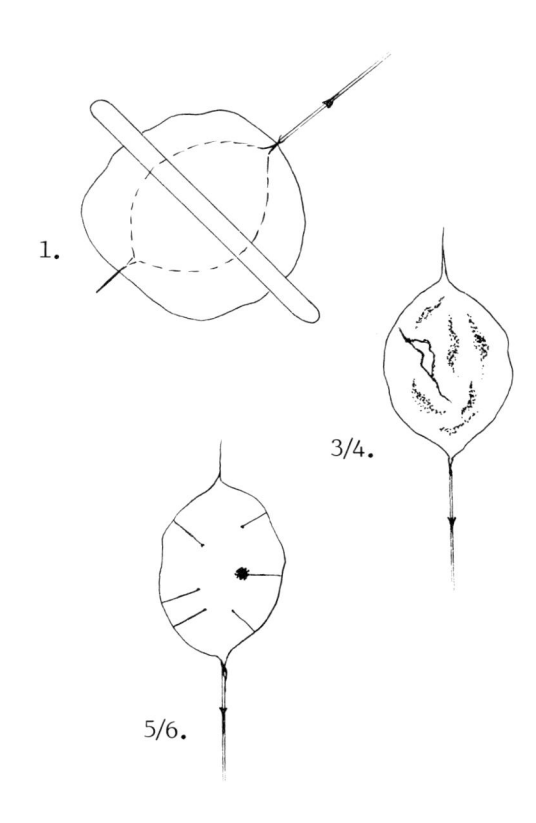

1.

3/4.

5/6.

1. Roll out a small piece of white paste until <u>very</u> thin, then roll again and again until almost transparent.
Place the wire circle on the board then lay the paste <u>on top</u> of the wire and roll with a small rolling pin until the wire cuts through the paste. Carefully remove excess paste.

NOTE: If the paste is fairly soft, it will stick to the frame without any moisture, however, if the paste is dry, it may be necessary to put a touch of gum glue onto the wire. Do not overdo this.

2. Lift the Honesty head very carefully from the board with a fine spatula.

3. Press onto the veiner to make an uneven surface then very gently twist the frame to give it 'movement' but do not loosen the paste. Leave to dry.

4. To make damaged Honesty, leave to dry for only a minute or two, resting the septum on a soft pad, press a sharp blade into the paste to 'tear' a jagged area.

5. Brush septum with fine white shimmer powder.
Draw very fine seed stalks with a brush or dark brown drawing pen, as illustrated.
Mark these seed stalks on both sides of the septum.

6. Sometimes the seeds do not develop. These stay on the surface as very tiny brown 'dots' and can be drawn with the same brown brush or pen.

7. Brush the edges of the tears with dark brown.

UNPEELED HONESTY

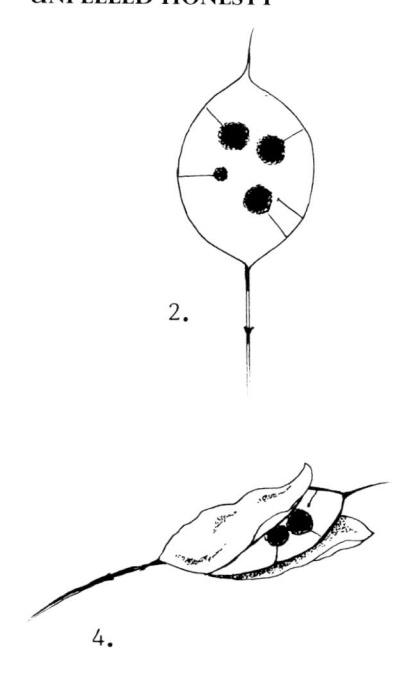

2.

4.

1. To make your Honesty spray more realistic, add at least one head with the two outer layers intact.

Make the white septum as above but do not vein or twist the wire frame.

2. Brush with white shimmer powder, paint seed stalks and then paint full-sized seeds as shown and leave to dry.

3. Colour paste <u>very</u> light grey/brown.
Roll out paste and cut out two shapes using a spare wire frame which should be the same size as the prepared white layer. Remove paste from the frame.

4. Vein both shapes on the mould then paint a narrow band of gum glue around the edges of the lower part of the shapes and set in place on each side of the dry white septum, easing them away from the surface so that the white layer and the seeds can be seen. Leave to dry.

5. Using a flat brush and hardly any powder colour, brush the surface of both outer layers with cream, brown and even a touch of black on the edges, but be careful not to over-colour; these layers need to look very pale and fragile.

HONESTY

ASSEMBLY

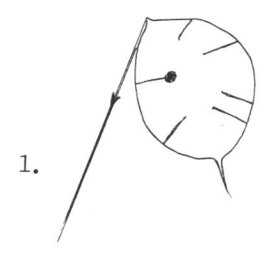

1. Bend each Honesty head precisely below the frame. Also draw the head slightly forward.

2. Using tiny slivers of beige tape, twist one or two 'fronds' about $1/4$ to $1/2$ inch (6 to 12mm) long.

3. With quarter-width beige tape, attach 2 or 3 'fronds' to the tip of a full-length 24 gauge white wire and tape down a few turns.

4. Join in one Honesty head with the stalk about $1\frac{1}{2}$ inches (3.5cm) long..

5. Tape down a little and join in another head.

6. Construct several individual stalks, each with several heads, then join two or more long stalks together until the required spray has been made.
NOTE: Add the broken heads and the unpeeled head where they will show to best advantage.
Your Honesty is most advantageously seen as a background to other seasonal flowers. See cover picture.

Hydrangea

Nothing of the season left, no fragrance to be found
Winter's frozen fingers tighten all around
The faded, shaded colours of hydrangea's dying flowers
Bring back lovely memories of summer's shining hours.

The hydrangea can be found in many lovely hues, especially in autumn and winter when the true colours fade and change to beautiful muted shades. The flowers may be used in many ways: in group of about 25 with or without leaves, as a focal point; in groups of between 3 and 10 florets together as secondary sprays or even individual florets as filler flowers.

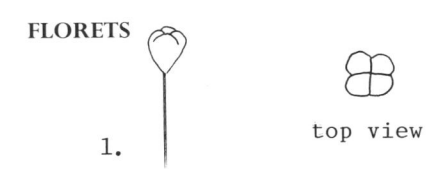

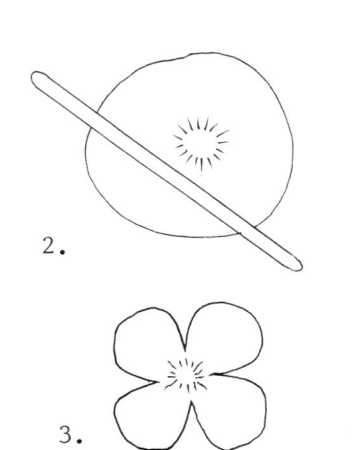

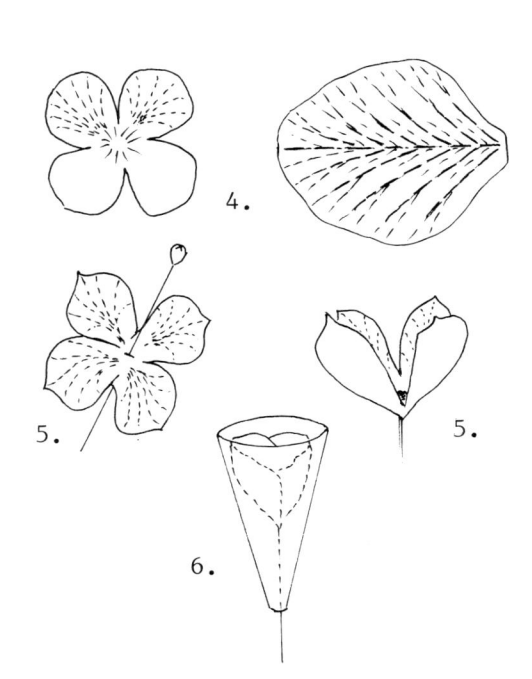

FLORETS

1.

top view

2.

3.

4.

5.   5.

6.

1. In the centre of each hydrangea floret is a tiny bud. This is actually the flower, whilst what we think of as the petals are bracts whose only function is to attract insects to the flower. This centre bud may be made by wrapping a tiny piece of white paste around the head of a large white stamen, then marking a cross on the top to represent the four unopened petals. Alternatively, use large white pointed stamens with the tip cut off, leaving a small 'knobbly' head. Cut off the unused head at the other end of the stamen cotton. Dip stamen head and cotton stem into liquid colour, to match the chosen colour of the floret.

NB: Choose stamens with stiff cotton stems otherwise the flower will not be adequately supported.
You could, of course, use short pieces of white 33 gauge wire.

2. Colour paste as required. use light cream for dried flowers as this gives a soft foundation, and very pale blue or pink for the fresh ones. Further powder colouring is detailed below.
Roll out paste to 1mm thick. Cut off a small piece, then, using a small rolling pin, continue to roll all round the edges leaving a tiny 'pimple' in the centre. The paste must be very fine.

3. Cut out the hydrangea flower with the 'pimple' in the centre, using the David Wregg cutter or a large 4-petalled daphne cutter. It should not be necessary to refine the petal edges if the paste has been rolled out sufficiently, but broaden each petal slightly.

4. Press each of the four petals onto the tip of a small JEM orchid petal veiner. Place the flower onto the firm side of a Cel Pad and press the centre of each petal with a ball tool to cup slightly. This will effectively press out some of the veining which would otherwise be a little too strong.

5. Pass a fine sewing needle right through the centre of the flower, then pull through one of the stamens which should be moistened very, very lightly. Pull the stamen until it nestles well down into the paste and at the same time, pinching the paste at the back of the flower. Gently pinch the tip of each petal into shape.

6. Some of the florets, notably those near the centre of the spray, may be slightly closed. To encourage these into shape, pull the flower through a small flower former, or the wide end of a piping nozzle.

Let all florets dry thoroughly before attempting to colour.

COLOURING DRIED HYDRANGEA

Brush the florets with powder colours from the following range:

Sugar Flair: Plum, violet, jade, ice blue, or cornflower.
Squires Kitchen: Hydrangea, blue grass, rose or thrift.
Or indeed, any other colours which suit your colour scheme.

COLOURING DYING HYDRANGEA

Pre-colour paste very light green, then brush plum or rose powder colour on the edges. Some florets will be almost all red and some still all green. Ensure that you have a good variety.

COLOURING FRESH HYDRANGEA

Having pre-coloured the paste in pale base shades, build up a pretty range of tints as required.

NOTE: Powder colour these very delicate florets with great care. Use a flat brush and work gently from the edges with every stroke.

LEAVES

(Leaves are not required with dried hydrangea).

Use large rose leaf cutters and fresh green paste. Make the leaves following the instructions on page 10.
Diamond Paste and Mould Co. make hydrangea leaf veiners in two sizes.

ASSEMBLY

1. Tape 5 or 6 florets together with their heads level.
The stems should be at least one inch (2.5cm) long.

2. Join in one 24 gauge wire.

3. Continue to add the outer florets, all on the same spot, then tape down the wire.

4. Tape the leaves into small sprays, if used and attach behind the flowers.

40

HYDRANGEA

IVY AND INSECTS

A secret world this ancient wall, curtained with evergreen
Part the stems to peer inside at the hidden dusty scene.
Rain never seems to penetrate the spider-cobwebbed cracks
It's only elves and fairies that this magic garden lacks.

The ivy berries shown here are at the stage between flowers and ripe black fruit. They can be used as an interesting addition to your wild flower arrangement, with or without leaves.
The insects are just for fun and are not meant to be insectually correct!!!

IVY BERRIES

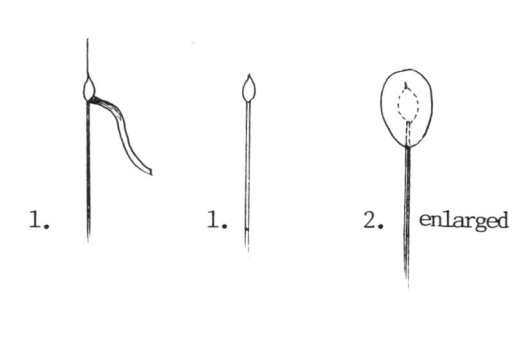

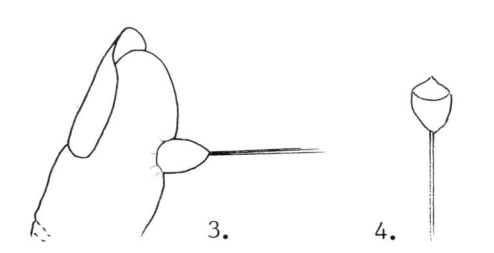

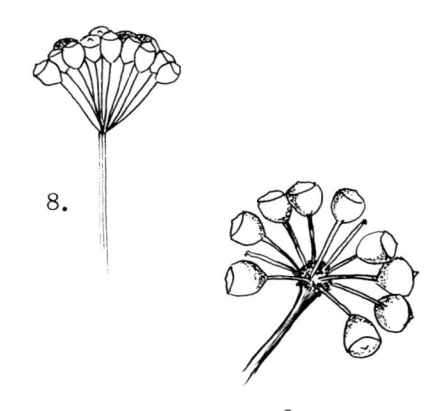

1. Cut 15 x 3 inch (7.5cm) pieces of dark green 33 gauge wire. Join dark green stem tape which has been cut into 1/8 widths, just below the tip of the wire. Bind a few times to make a VERY small pad, then continue to tape down the wire for half its length.
Cut off the tip of the wire so that it is no more than 1mm above the taped pad.

2. Colour paste light olive green.
Roll a ball of paste about the size of a glass-headed pin. It is important not to make these berries too large.
Moisten the pad and insert into the base of the berry.
The tip of the wire must not protrude.

3. Shape the paste as shown, then press the top of the berry against the soft part of your thumb. This will effectively flatten the top and will allow the tip of the wire to push up a tiny point without actually breaking through, though this cannot always be avoided as it will depend upon the texture of your paste.

4. Using a thin drinking straw or a size 4 piping nozzle, lightly indent a tiny circle into the top of the berry around the point. Do not press too hard.

5. Gently re-roll the sides of the berry to make sure that it is not too wide as it may have been pushed out by the pressure of the straw or nozzle.

6. Leave to dry then brush the top with a touch of yellow powder colour or just a breath of chestnut. Also brush over the edges of the circle with shadow green.

7. Dip berries into half glaze and leave to dry thoroughly.

8. Using twig or olive tape, tape the berries together in small groups. Each stem is 2/5 inch (1cm) long.
There are about 15 berries in one full head, but some do drop off during the season, so use only as many as is necessary to make the head look right.

9. Once all the berries are taped together, open them out to form a little ball.
With 1/4-width stem tape, bind through and around the base of the berry wires to form a small irregularly shaped base.
Scratch this base with a needle to roughen it up a little and to eliminate the overlaps of the taping.
Polish the main stem with a smooth metal tool to make it shine.

IVY AND INSECTS

43

LEAVES

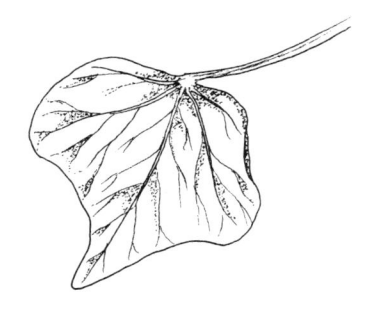

1. The leaves which grow with these berries are not very pointed. The general shape is shown in the illustration.
Make leaves following the instructions on page 10, using light green paste.

2. Mix holly/ivy powder colour with a little white fat and use this to brush over the front of the leaves, then scratch the veins with a cocktail stick, following the pattern of a real leaf if possible.

Glaze in the usual way and 'move' edges as soon as possible.

INSECTS

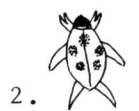

1. Colour paste dark brown or as required for the legs of your chosen insect.
Roll out paste quite thinly and cut out the 'under carriage' with the Orchard 6-petalled cutter No. N8.
Lay 'under carriage' on board and push the two front legs forward, cutting the tips with a sharp blade for the pincers.
The middle and back legs go backwards.

2. Roll a small oval ball of coloured paste for the body.
Put a dot of gum glue into the centre of the under carriage and set the body in place.
Immediately mark a deep line down the length of the body with a sharp blade to divide for the wing casings.
Make a line above this for the head.

3. Paint markings on body as required.
Leave to dry.
Glaze body with a brush made by twisting a small piece of kitchen towel, to avoid ruining your brushes.

SUGGESTIONS:

Ladybird - Red body, black spots.
Colorado beetle - Yellow body, brown stripes.
Soldier beetle (blood sucker) - Red/brown long body, segmented.
Spider - Light brown body, brown pattern. (should have 8 legs, but who's counting?).
Nightmare beetle - Pink body, blue stripes, green spots!!

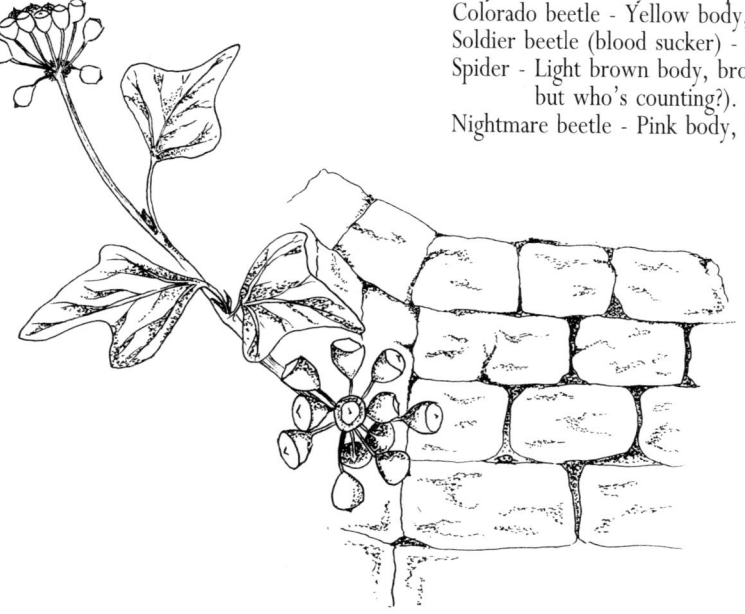

LARCH CONES

Walk the quiet forest aisles beneath the arching trees
Breathe the good sweet smell of pine that comes upon the breeze.
Gather golden fir cones to kindle on the hearth
And recreate your memories down nature's scented path.

The larch is a deciduous conifer, losing its needles in winter. However, the cones stay on the tree for several years after the seeds have fallen. Make bare twigs with cones to give elegance and shape to your arrangement, or add colour and softness with the fresh green needles.

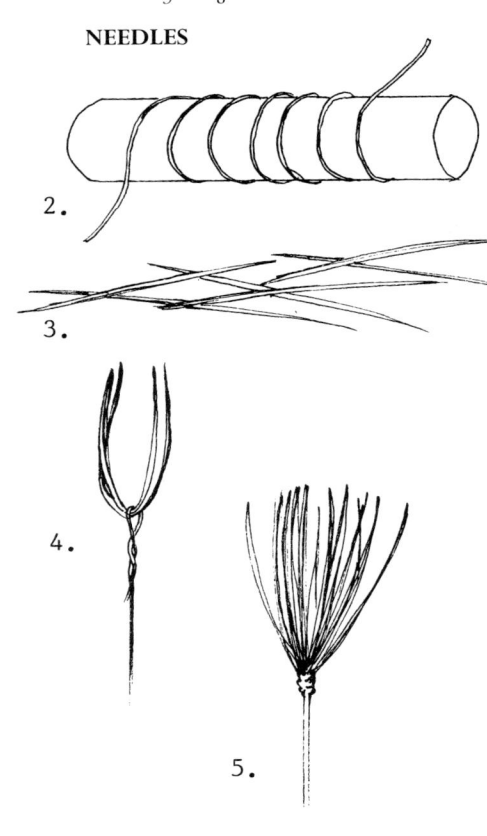

NEEDLES

1. Cut a one yard (1 metre) piece of green stem tape and shred it into four lengths. Twist each quarter-width tightly into 'fronds', stretching as you go so that the final frond is as long as it can be.

2. Bind each length around a medium rolling pin and roll firmly on a board to flatten the twisted tape.

3. Measure lengths for the needles as required (see below) and BREAK off. Do not CUT. This will ensure that the tips will be pointed and fine.

4. Take 2 x 2 inch (5cm) pieces and fold in half to make four needles. Make a hook on a half length dark green 28 gauge wire and hook over the folded needles. Twist wire very tightly two or three times to secure.

5. Using twig coloured quarter-width stem tape, bind around the base of the needles to make a very small pad for the leaf base.
Continue to tape down the wire for $1/2$ inch (12mm) only.

6. Still using two inch pieces of twisted tape, repeat the above, making small groups of needles as follows:
One more with two fronds. (four needles).
One with three fronds. (six needles).
One with four fronds. (eight needles).
One with five fronds. (ten needles).
Complete the leaf bases as at 5. above.

7. Using $2\frac{1}{2}$ inch (6cm) pieces of twisted tape, make these groups of needles:
Two with two fronds.
Two with three fronds.
Three with four fronds.
Three with five fronds.

8. Using $3\frac{1}{2}$ inch (9cm) pieces of twisted tape, make ten groups of needles with approximately eight fronds. (16 needles).
With these latter groups make the leaf bases slightly larger and texture with a strong needle to make the taping look like woody bark. (See twigs and branches - basic method. page 11).

9. Bend the wire immediately below each leaf base.

NOTE: There will be a number of needles used singly on the tip of each twig to represent the newest growth. Prepare tape as above and break off 20 or more two inch (5cm) pieces in readiness for the assembly.

Also make some single needles in beige or light brown tape for the dead twig. Brush the tips with chestnut powder colour.

OLD CONES

1.

2.

3.

N7
N6
N5
small space
N5
small spacer
N5
large spacer
N6
small spacer
N6
large spacer
N7
small spacer
N7
N8
cone

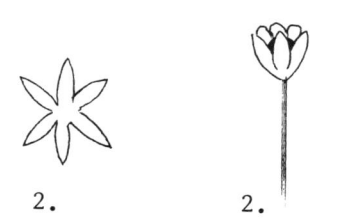

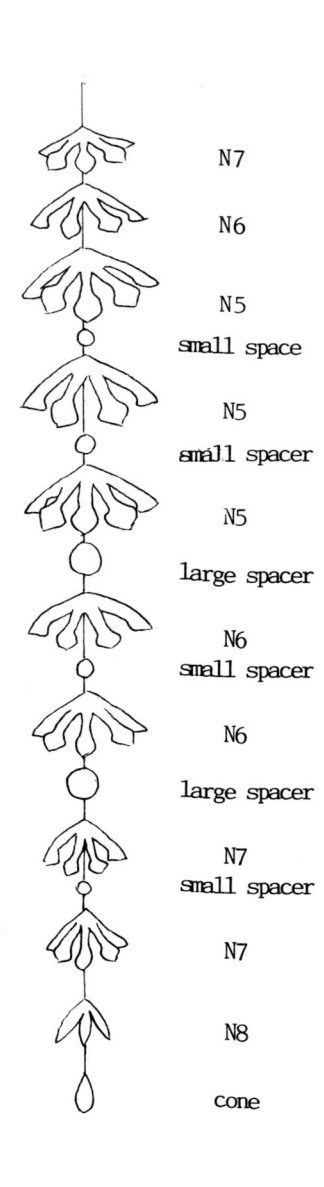

1. Colour a small piece of paste bullrush brown. Add plenty of white paste until you have a lighter brown then add just a touch of black paste colour to make a rather dull grey/brown. Hook half-length 26 gauge wires and make a very small oval cone on the tip of each.

2. To make the cone scales use Orchard six-petalled flower cutters sizes N5 to N8.

Roll out paste thinly and cut out one N8 flower. Place on the firm side of a Cel pad and thin and spread the petals (scales) with a bodkin or small ball tool. Moisten cone very lightly and set the N8 flower in place with the scales drawn forward over the cone.

3. With the paste not too thin, cut out an N7 flower. Thin and spread the tip of the scales to the shape illustrated. Set in place over the N8 flower, allowing the scales to sit slightly away from the first round.

4. Roll a very tiny ball of paste and slip onto the wire. Moisten only the underside of this 'spacer' to stick it to the previous round of scales. Push well down so that the spacer is not too high.

5. Repeat the N7 scales as at 3. above. Attach to the previous round with moisture only on the top of the spacer, not on the scales.

Continue as follows, allowing a little space between each layer of scales so that the cone looks dry and mature:

6. Make a large spacer and add an N6 flower.

7. Make a small spacer and add another N6 flower.

8. Make a large spacer and add an N5 flower.

9. Make a small spacer and add another N5 flower.

10. Repeat 9. once more.

11. Add an N6 flower with NO spacer.

12. Add an N7 flower with NO spacer.

NOTE: The above instructions will give you a full-sized cone with 10 layers of scales. Make smaller cones simply by leaving out two of the N5 layers. (8 layers of scales).

13. Using twig coloured stem tape, make a small knotty pad behind the cone and tape down the wire for $1/2$ inch (12mm) only.

14. Leave the cone to dry then brush with shadow green powder colour (see glossary). This will make the cones appear to be old and weather beaten.

<u>YOUNG CONES</u>
1. Colour paste as above but without the black.
Add chestnut or orange paste colour to make a warmer brown.

Make the cones as above but allow the scales to rest slightly closer upon each other.

2. When dry, brush neat brown paste colour onto the edges of the scales.

3. Make knotty pads behind the cones as before.

LARCH CONES

OLD BUDS

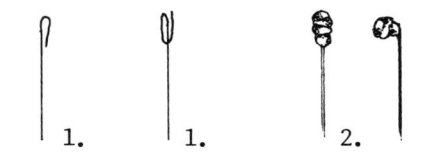

1. 1. 2.

ASSEMBLY

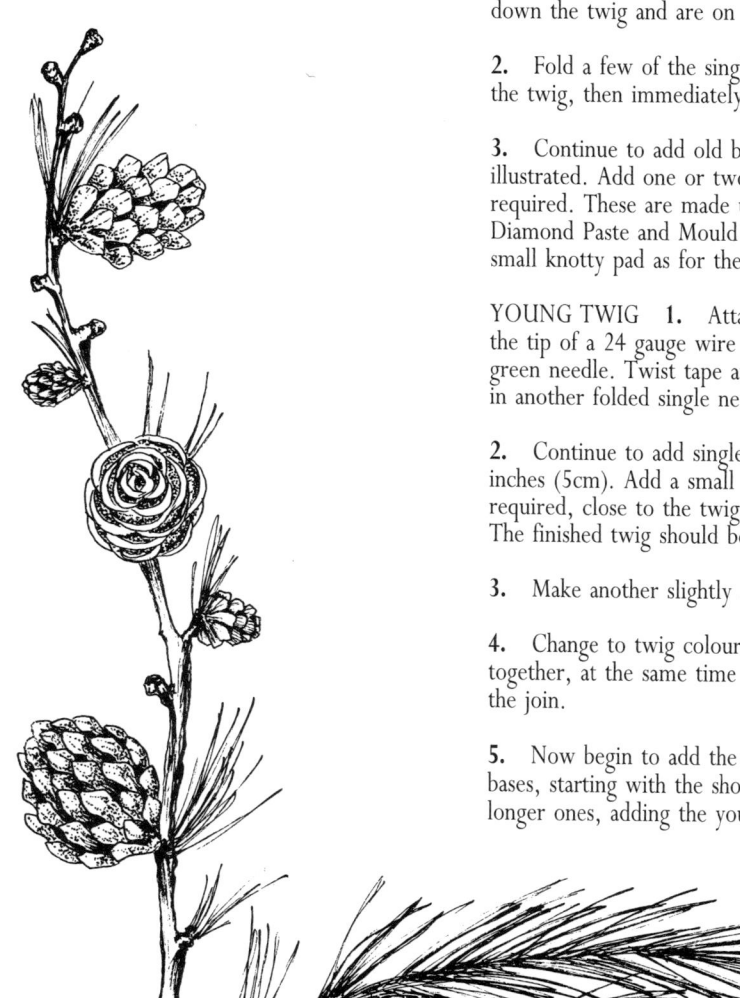

1. Use any odd pieces of wire, $2\frac{1}{2}$ to 3 inches (6 to 8cm) long. Make a small hook at one end and then double it over.

2. With quarter-width twig coloured stem tape, bind the double hooks to make a small fat pad with a stubby tip. (not pointed). Tape down for $\frac{1}{2}$ inch (12mm) and bend wire below bud as shown.

OLD TWIG **1.** Using quarter-width twig coloured stem tape, attach one old bud to the tip of a 24 gauge wire and tape down for about $\frac{1}{4}$ inch (6mm). Add another old bud, tape down a little and add another one just below.

NOTE: These old buds are all that is left when the groups of needles and cones fall off. They are spaced at irregular intervals down the twig and are on all sides.

2. Fold a few of the single brown needles in half and tape onto the twig, then immediately attach an old cone.

3. Continue to add old buds, dead needles and old cones as illustrated. Add one or two brown underdeveloped cones if required. These are made using the small cone mould from Diamond Paste and Mould Company. Insert wire and make a very small knotty pad as for the full-sized cone.

YOUNG TWIG **1.** Attach quarter-width BEIGE stem tape to the tip of a 24 gauge wire and immediately tape in a folded single green needle. Twist tape around wire just once or twice and tape in another folded single needle.

2. Continue to add single needles down the twig for about 2 inches (5cm). Add a small green underdeveloped cone, if required, close to the twig and continue with the single needles. The finished twig should be about five inches (12.5cm) long.

3. Make another slightly shorter twig.

4. Change to twig coloured stem tape and join the two twigs together, at the same time adding a small young cone to disguise the join.

5. Now begin to add the groups of green needles with their leaf bases, starting with the short needles and gradually introducing the longer ones, adding the young cones at intervals.

MICHAELMAS DAISIES

The garden sleeps and dreams now that the season's work is ended
A sense of peace and idleness has all the world befriended
The purple daisies that are left look tattered and forlorn
Only the berries shine for joy and wait for Christmas morn.

Any daisy made in sugar has a built-in problem, the delicacy of the fine petals. The michaelmas daisy is no exception, but it is well worth the effort. The secret is to make the complete flower without allowing the petals to dry before adding the calyx. Use as a colourful secondary flower in your arrangements. Pink, red, white, blue, mauve and purple cultivars are available.

CLOSED FLOWER BUD

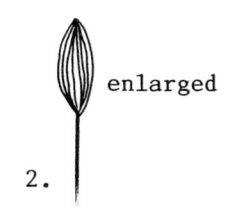

1. Prepare paste in your chosen colour.
Tape a light green 30 gauge wire with green stem tape and make a hook.
Shape a small cone, no more than 1/4 inch (6mm) long and insert the hooked wire.

2. Using a sharp blade, mark the bud with several lines to look like closed petals.
Leave to dry.

CALYX

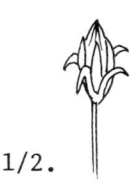

1. Colour paste mid-green.
Roll out quite thinly and cut out a daisy using the FMM D1 cutter.
Cut each petal in half, lengthways.

2. Slightly cup the centre of the calyx, moisten lightly and set in place around the prepared bud.
Allow most of the sepals to sit close to the bud, but lift back about five, as shown.

OPENING BUD

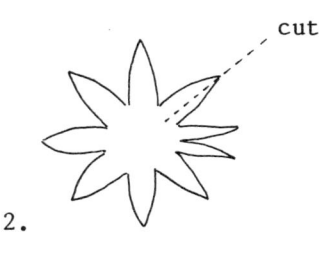

1. Tape wire and prepare centre as for the closed bud.

2. Roll out the coloured paste very thinly and cut out an FMM D2 daisy.
Cut petals in half.

3. Lay flower on the palm of the hand or on the soft side of a Cel pad and stroke each petal from the centre to the tip with a size 13 tapestry needle or narrow veining tool.
NOTE: The pressure needs to be as strong as your paste will allow, in order to vein and shape the petals. If the paste is a bit soft, allow the flower to 'rest' for a few moments before veining.

4. Ball the centre of the flower and set in place around the bud, allowing most of the petals to sit away slightly.

5. Complete the calyx as before.
It is important to make the calyx before the flower dries or the petals may break.

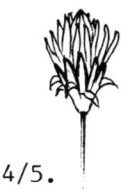

OPEN FLOWER

1.

2.

cut --
3.

3.

4.

LEAVES

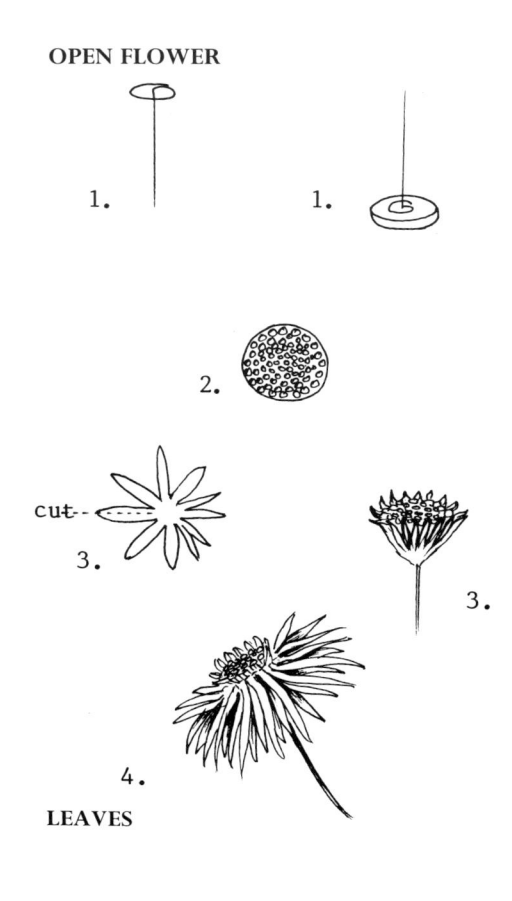

ASSEMBLY

1. Tape wire as above.
Make a medium 'ski stick' on the wire (see glossary).
Roll a small ball of lemon yellow paste. (size 4 or 5 on the Cel size guide).
Place ball on a board, moisten the top of the ski stick and press onto the ball of paste so that it 'oozes' through the twisted wires and becomes firmly attached.

2. Immediately indent the middle area with a size 1 piping nozzle, then finish with size 2 nozzle around the edge.
This marking represents the tips of the stamens.
Leave to dry thoroughly.

3. Roll out yellow paste very thinly and cut out an FMM D1 daisy.
Cut each petal into several 'blades'.
Cup centre, moisten and set in place so that the tips just show outside the embossed middle.

4. Cut out, vein and set in place two rounds of coloured daisy using the FMM D3 daisy cutter.
NB: Smaller flowers may be made, using the FMM D2 cutter.

5. Complete the calyx as before.
NOTE: Some mature flowers may have petals which fall back a little. These, however, will be particularly fragile.

1. Roll a tiny sausage of green paste and insert a fine, uncovered rose wire.
Roll with a small rolling pin to make a flat leaf, no more than $\frac{1}{2}$ inch (12mm) long.
Bend the wire at the base of the leaf and tape close to the flower stem, just below the flower.

2. Make a few more leaves up to 1 inch (2.5cm) long and attach to the flower stem as shown.

1. Tape several flowers together with their heads fairly level.

2. Add some leaves, made as above but slightly longer, below the joint of the flower stems.

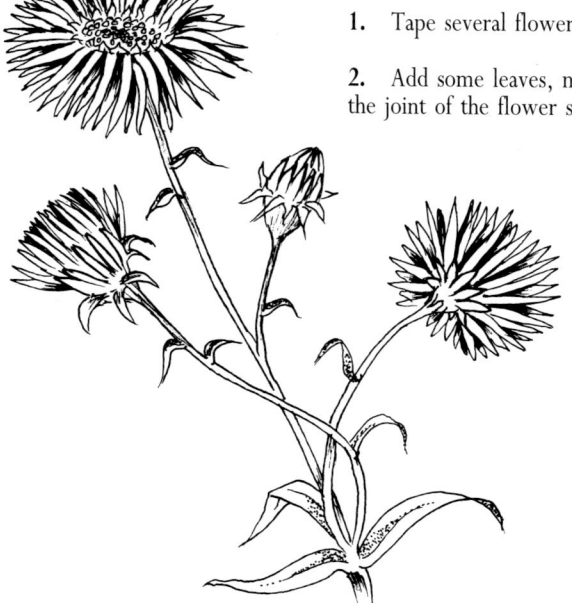

MICHAELMAS DAISY

MIMOSA

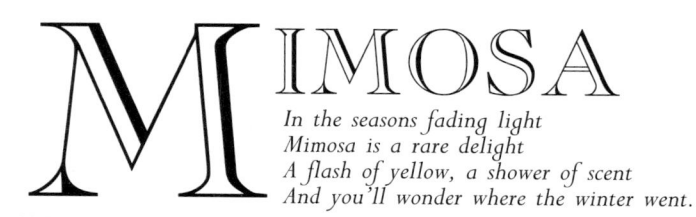

*In the seasons fading light
Mimosa is a rare delight
A flash of yellow, a shower of scent
And you'll wonder where the winter went.*

This beautiful, highly scented flower is native to Australia where it is called acacia, to Africa where it is the thorn tree and to England where it is mimosa. There are hundreds of varieties and I have chosen one with feathery leaves because they are so attractive and easy to make and could be used on their own to complement any floral spray with or without the flowers shown here.

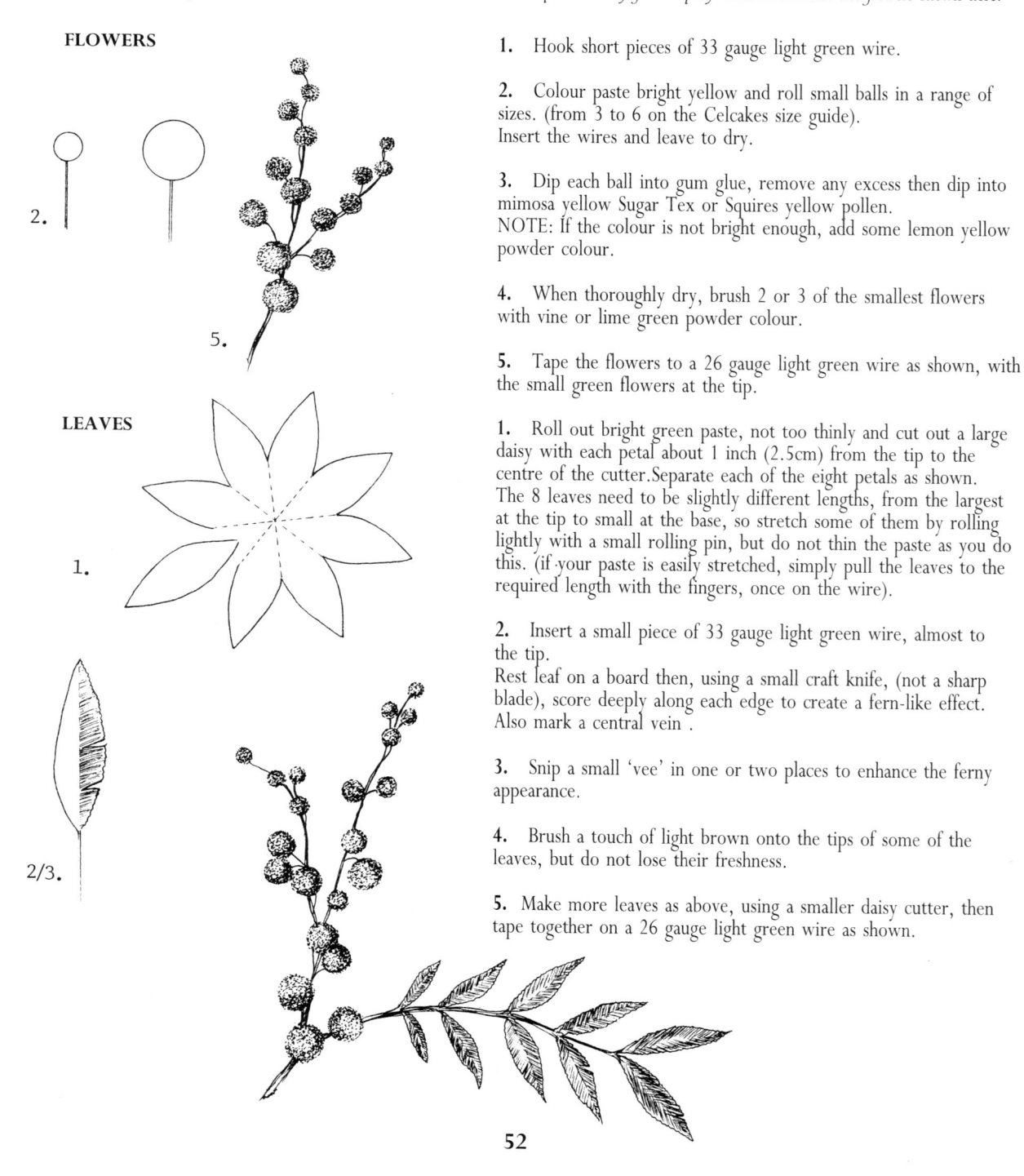

FLOWERS

1. Hook short pieces of 33 gauge light green wire.

2. Colour paste bright yellow and roll small balls in a range of sizes. (from 3 to 6 on the Celcakes size guide).
Insert the wires and leave to dry.

3. Dip each ball into gum glue, remove any excess then dip into mimosa yellow Sugar Tex or Squires yellow pollen.
NOTE: If the colour is not bright enough, add some lemon yellow powder colour.

4. When thoroughly dry, brush 2 or 3 of the smallest flowers with vine or lime green powder colour.

5. Tape the flowers to a 26 gauge light green wire as shown, with the small green flowers at the tip.

LEAVES

1. Roll out bright green paste, not too thinly and cut out a large daisy with each petal about 1 inch (2.5cm) from the tip to the centre of the cutter. Separate each of the eight petals as shown. The 8 leaves need to be slightly different lengths, from the largest at the tip to small at the base, so stretch some of them by rolling lightly with a small rolling pin, but do not thin the paste as you do this. (if your paste is easily stretched, simply pull the leaves to the required length with the fingers, once on the wire).

2. Insert a small piece of 33 gauge light green wire, almost to the tip.
Rest leaf on a board then, using a small craft knife, (not a sharp blade), score deeply along each edge to create a fern-like effect. Also mark a central vein.

3. Snip a small 'vee' in one or two places to enhance the ferny appearance.

4. Brush a touch of light brown onto the tips of some of the leaves, but do not lose their freshness.

5. Make more leaves as above, using a smaller daisy cutter, then tape together on a 26 gauge light green wire as shown.

MIMOSA

MISTLETOE

Though fingers freeze when when the east wind blows
A Christmas tree in a window glows
Promising pleasures I wouldn't miss
That's why I'm standing poised for a kiss!

The mistletoe, with its translucent white berries makes a simple spray for your Christmas cake, with or without other foliage.

BERRIES

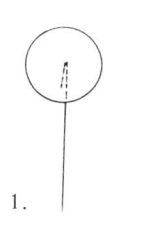

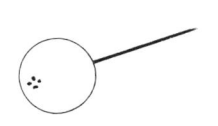

1.

1. Hook short pieces of 33 gauge light green wire.
Roll small balls of white paste and insert the hooked wire.
Close the hole where the wire went in and re-shape the berry to a good round ball.

2. Put a drop of green liquid colour into a dish and add a little water to dilute.
Using a fine brush, put a touch of colour onto the berry at the point where the wire enters.
Do not overdo this.

3. Dip the tip of a fine sewing needle into neat dark brown paste colour, then make a group of four tiny holes into the berry as shown. Be careful not to smudge the dots.

4. Leave to dry then dip the berries into half glaze. They should have a sheen rather than a hard shine.

5. When thoroughly dry, brush berries with <u>very</u> pale vine green powder.

LEAVES

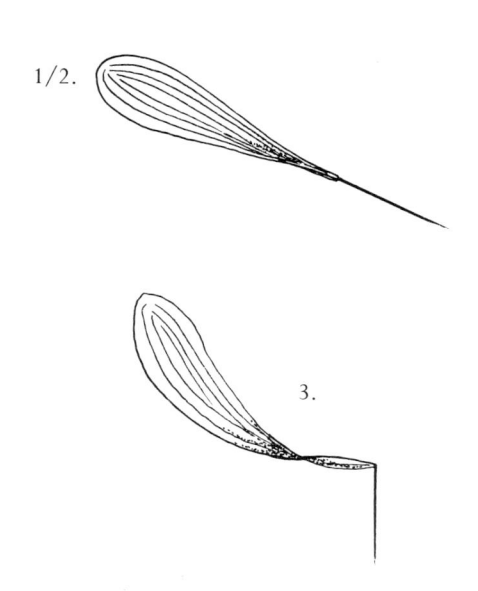

1/2.

3.

1. Mistletoe leaves are long and very slim.
Use mistletoe leaf cutters or, as I do, a slim orchid petal cutter.

Colour paste a light, fresh, yellowy green and make leaves following the instructions on page 10.

2. The veins are very light indeed and are linear.
If veiners are not available, use a corn cob.

3. Brush a little moss green powder colour at the base of the leaves before glazing, then curve them into the characteristic shape shown.

MISTLETOE

ASSEMBLY

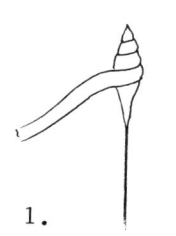

1. Between each pair of leaves there is a triangular bud. Bind quarter-width light green tape to the tip of a 26 gauge light green hooked wire until you have the shape shown.

2. Bend the wires of two of the leaves and attach on either side of the bud.
Continue to bind tape several times to thicken the stem below the leaves and then tape down the wire.

3. Attach as many pairs of leaves as required, and then add the berries singly or in small clusters of two or three, with very short stalks.

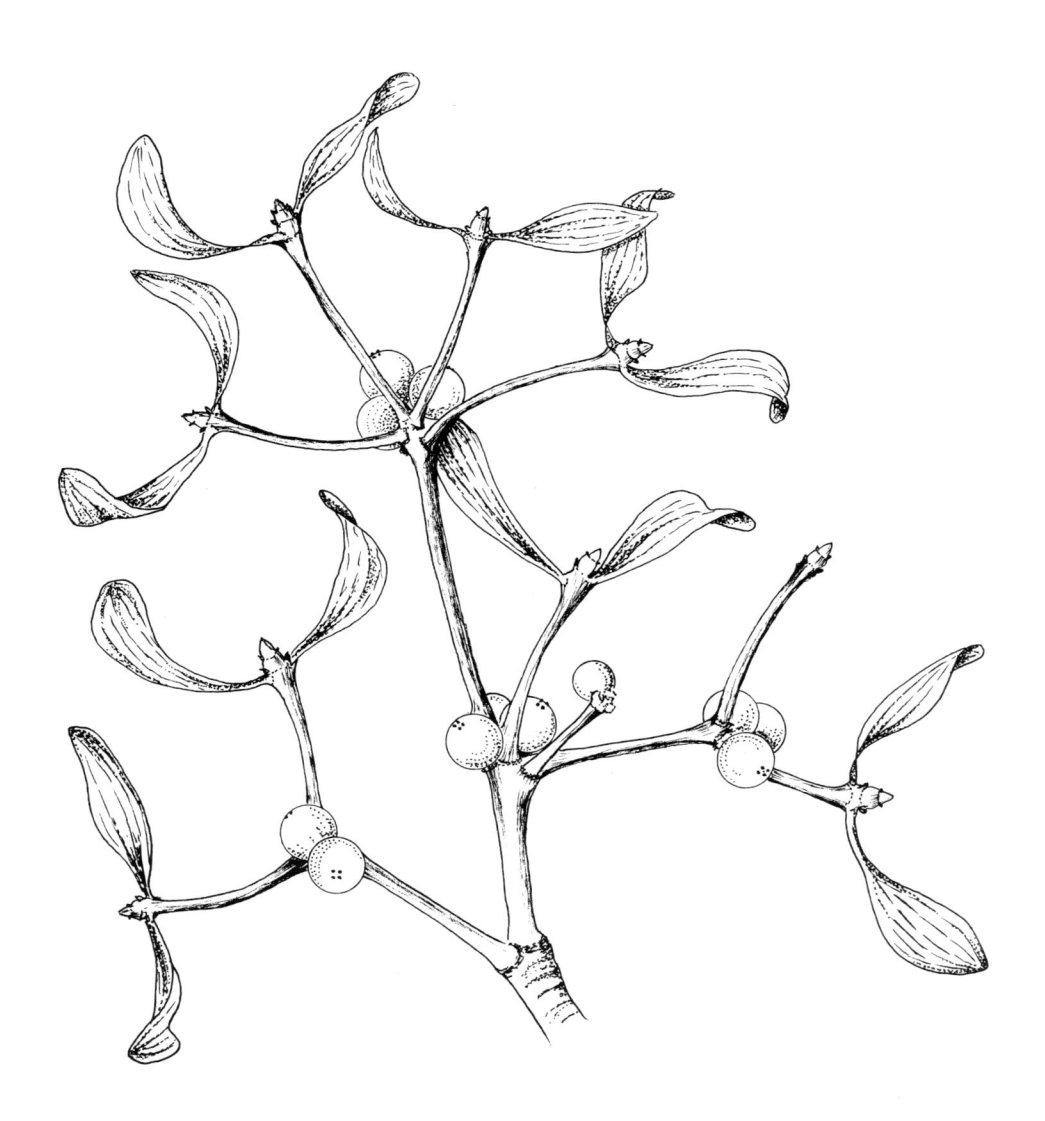

1.

OLD MAN'S BEARD

OLD MAN'S BEARD

Winter hedgerows love to whisper
Telling tales of seasons lost
Garlanded with fluffy seedheads,
Silver whiskers rhimed with frost.

The proper name for this interesting plant is Traveller's Joy. It is a wild clematis, but it is the fruit for which it is best known. The long, grey, hairy plumes, in dense clusters, persisting through the winter, give rise to the name Old Man's Beard. This may also be used as the seedhead for the popular cultivated clematis when it will add an unusual touch guaranteed to catch the eye.

SEEDHEAD (WHISKERS)

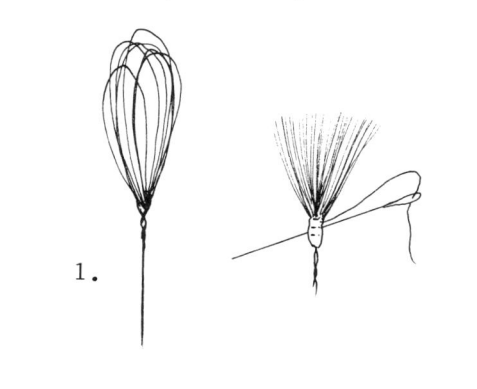

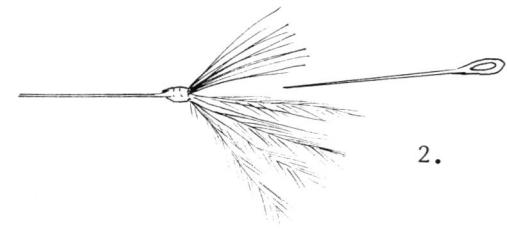

1.

2.

3/5.

1. Use white silk thread if possible, but any thread will do. Twist thread around two fingers about 80 times.
Hook a 30 gauge white wire through the loops and twist wire to hold threads.
Using a fine needle, stitch through a few times, just above the wire. This will ensure that the threads do not divide into two parts.
Trim to $1\frac{1}{4}$-$1\frac{1}{2}$ inches (3-4cm) then, holding the threads tightly in a bunch, rub the tips with an emery board to fluff them out.

2. Lay the seed head on a firm surface. (not your board, as you may scratch it).
Using a very strong sharp needle, 'scratch' the threads from the wire end to the tips many, many times, until gradually, they separate and begin to look like whiskers. Better still, use a fine Kemper texturing tool.
If you look at real Old Man's Beard, you will see that each 'frond' actually looks like a miniature feather!

NOTE: If you miss some of the threads, and they look thick, don't worry, as when the seed head is damp, it can look quite 'clumpy' and untidy, so a more natural effect can be obtained by mixing a variety of thicknesses.

3. Using quarter-width twig stem tape, tape the stitched area below the head and then on down the wire.

4. Mix some white powder with a tiny touch of black and brown to make a <u>very</u> light off-white colour. Do not make the colour too strong or your whiskers will look dirty.
Brush whiskers with the powder, adding just a touch of light green in the centre of the head.

5. Mix a little light brown paste with a few drops of alcohol to make a thick paste.
Use this to brush at the base of the whiskers to represent the seeds from which the whiskers grow.
Leave to dry.

LEAVES

Usually, by the time the seed head has developed, the leaves will have fallen, however, for added interest, make a few leaves, either green or brown and crumpled.
Use a plain leaf cutter, with the pointed end at the tip of the leaf. Follow the instructions on page 10, using a clematis leaf veiner. Cut notches at the side of the leaf as shown.

ASSEMBLY

Tape one, two or three seed heads together at the tip of a 24 gauge wire, using twig stem tape and following the instructions on page 11 for making a smooth twig.

Add leaves.

SPINDLEBERRIES

As gloomy winter deepens
Leaving all forlorn
Spindleberries spark with fire
To glorify the dawn.

The spindle tree is deciduous, with startling orange-red autumn tints. After leaf fall, there is a second display - twigs studded with brilliant clusters of seed capsules which last well past Christmas. Here, the leaves and berries are shown growing together for a superb effect.

CLOSED SEED CAPSULES

1.

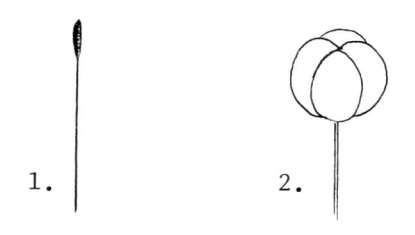

2.

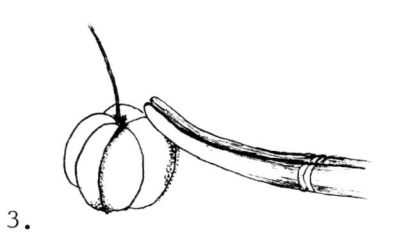

3.

1. Colour paste a pretty coral pink, using red and white with a touch of orange. Make a small hook on several quarter-length 33 gauge white wires. Cover hooks with a VERY tiny piece of the coral paste, barely covering them. Leave to dry.

2. Roll pea-sized piece of coral paste into a ball and insert the moistened paste-covered hook.
Mark a deep cross into to the top of the ball then continue the four cuts round the berry to the wire.
Go over the cuts again to ensure that the berry appears to be divided into four segments.

3. Using fine tweezers, pinch a very narrow ridge down each of the four segments. Pinch the wire end of the paste with tweezers to form a tiny uneven area to represent the old calyx.

4. Paint the old calyx and ½ inch (12mm) of the stem wire with neat reddish brown paste colour.
The seed capsules have a matt finish, but look a little fresher if lightly steamed.

OPEN SEED CAPSULES

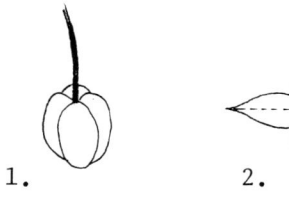

1.

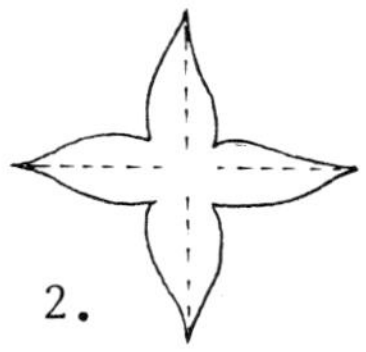

2.

3.

3.

1. Colour paste bright orange.
Form a slightly smaller four segmented berry as for the closed seed capsule, without the ridges.
Dip into confectioner's glaze and leave to dry thoroughly.

2. Roll out a small piece of coral paste quite thinly and cut out a large Daphne four-petalled flower or use a mini fuchsia which is a little longer.

3. Mark a vein down each of the four petals, to encourage a fold. Brush a narrow line of moisture down each cut on the orange berry and set the coral petals in place with the indented veins fitting into the moist grooves.
Push the petals deep into the grooves with a knife but be careful not to cut the petals in half, although a few split petals would be quite natural.
Ensure that the tips of the petals are well tucked underneath and stuck in the middle of the cross.
Lift the edges of the petals away from the orange berries.
Leave to dry and steam if desired.

4. Paint the stems as before.

SPINDLEBERRIES

LEAVES

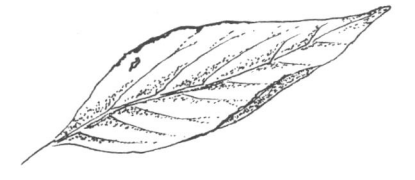

1. Colour paste light cream and make leaves on white 30 gauge half length wires.
Use slim plain leaf cutters in several sizes and a simple veiner such as a garden rose or a periwinkle.

2. As each leaf is made, brush with neat paste colours to ensure that the colours are very bright and strong:
Brush on lemon yellow with bright red at the tips and along the edges, merging the colours to make orange.
Some leaves may be yellow with green at the wire end and others may be all red.
Try to create an attractive assortment of leaves.

3. Glaze the leaves and when dry, brush on dark brown paste colour on the edges.
Make some interesting 'grotty bits' as these leaves are quite old.
Paint the stem wires with reddish brown as for the seed capsules.

ASSEMBLY

1. The berries and leaves all have short stems.
Tape three leaves together with brown tape for the tip of the spray.

2. Add leaves and berries as illustrated.

NOTE: One of the characteristics of this shrub is the 90° angle at which the side twigs grow from the main stem.
This can be rather 'stiff' looking and should be modified to suit your arrangement.

THISTLE

One day the winter snows will melt
The glens will sing with rain
Thistles sweet about my feet:
Scotland in bloom again.

Another idea for your Scottish celebration and a challenge for you. Did you ever think that you could make thistles entirely of sugar with not a single cotton thread in sight? Try this method and see how effective and easy it is. A word of caution though .... the flowers are very fragile and need careful handling.

FLOWER HEAD

Colour paste deep mauve with a touch of pink.

1. Tape half-length 24 gauge wires with dark green stem tape, then tape over again to make a fairly thick stem. Make a short hook at the tip.

2. Shape a small pea-sized piece of paste into a fat cone, not more than $2/5$ inch (1cm) long. Insert the hook and re-shape the cone with a slightly domed top. Check the length of the cone.
IMPORTANT NOTE: Do not make this cone too large or the petals will be too short.

3. With a sharp sewing needle, 'flick' up the surface of the top of the cone until it looks like the tips of many tiny petals.
Leave to dry thoroughly, overnight if possible.

4. Roll out paste very thinly and cut out a daisy using the FMM D2 cutter. Cut each petal into four. Thin the centre with a ball tool.

5. Lightly moisten the base of the cone and pull up the daisy to fit closely with the tips of the petals level with the top of the cone. Repeat with a second daisy.
NOTE: For small flowers two daisies should be sufficient, but for fuller flowers add one or two more, 'fluffing' out the tips as shown.

6. Roll a small ball of mauve paste. (size 4 on the Sugar Facts size guide, or a petit pois size).
Pull the wire through, moisten and press the ball firmly to the base of the flower head.
With the tip of a Honiton bobbin or similar pointed tool, roll over the join of the ball and the base of the flower to emphasise the shape and to secure well.
Leave to dry.

CALYX/BRACTS

1. Using green paste, cut out an FMM D2 daisy. The paste should not be too thin.
Do not cut the petals into four as for the flower head.
Thin the centre with a ball tool and set in place over the mauve ball.
Immediately roll the bracts to encourage them to shape over the ball and hide the join of the ball and the flower head.

2. Repeat with another D2 daisy, setting these bracts in between those of the first round.

3. Add a small ball of paste as a 'spacer' and mould until it is flat and close to the base of the previous layers.

4. Add one more D2 layer.

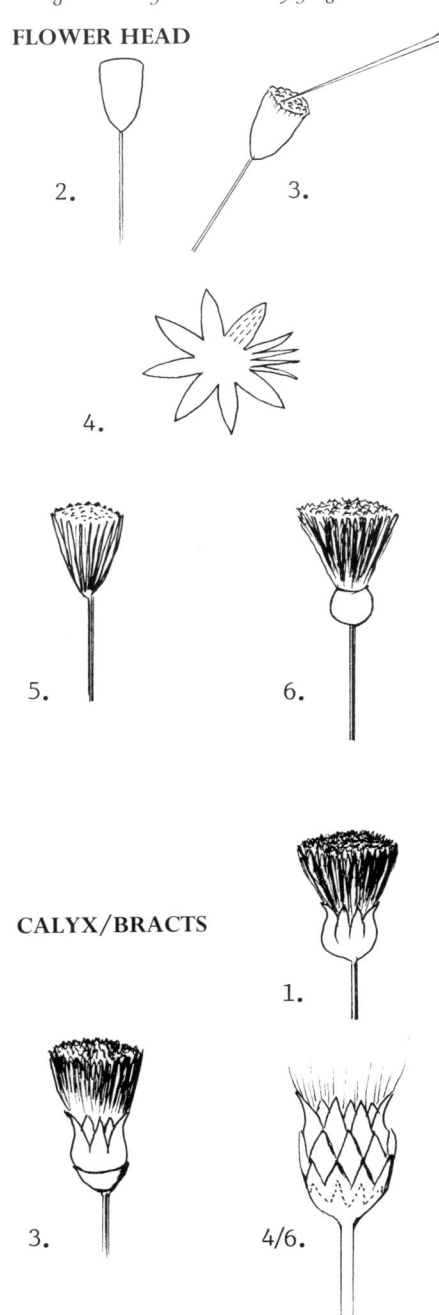

enlarged

CALYX/BRACTS (Continued)

5. Add one D1 daisy.

6. Immediately, whilst the paste is still soft, make tiny pointed snips into the base of each bract of the D1 daisy round, using very fine scissors. These represent the final layer of bracts.

COLOURING THE BRACTS: Using neat Heather colour Sugartint Droplets and a flat brush, paint the bracts with careful downward strokes so that you only colour the tips, leaving the area behind the bracts still green.

FLOWER HEAD GONE TO SEED

1. Make the flower head as above but use off-white paste.
Do not make the centre cone, just a very slim piece of paste to cover the hook of the wire, then add three layers of FMM D2 daisies.
Colour the base of each round of petals with a faint touch of brown powder, so that they appear to be dying.

2. Complete and colour the calyx/bracts as for the flower.

LEAVES

1. Use holly leaf cutters and dark green paste.
Roll out paste with a narrow vein up the centre.
Roll the paste <u>very</u> thinly on either side of the vein.
This is very important because the points must not be touched or they will not be 'prickly' enough for these very spiny leaves.

2. Insert a 30 gauge dark green wire and immediately s-t-r-e-t-c-h the leaf to lengthen it as much as possible, but do not break it.

3. Vein leaf with a veiner that doesn't have too much detail, such as a periwinkle or oak leaf.

4. Brush the front of the leaf with a shadow green powder colour (see glossary). Dip into half glaze, blot and leave to dry for only one or two minutes. As soon as it's possible to handle the leaf, twist and 'move' it into the shape required.

5. Make approximately one small, one medium and one large leaf for each flower.
Tape together as illustrated.

THISTLE

VANDA ORCHID

Winter ways are wonderful, though the foilage is lost
Flowers are now in hiding, afraid to face the frost.
Come into the greenhouse, it's warm and welcoming
Stay and watch the orchids grow until, once more, it's spring.

The variety of vanda orchid chosen here is the Rothschildiana with its unusual checkerboard veining. The real flower has no raised veins on its petals from which to mould a veiner so, ultimately, there was nothing for it but to hand-sculpt one. In order to obtain the right effect, the veins are impressed so that they are raised on the front of the petals and the colour brushed across the ridges. It may not be botanically correct, but it works!!

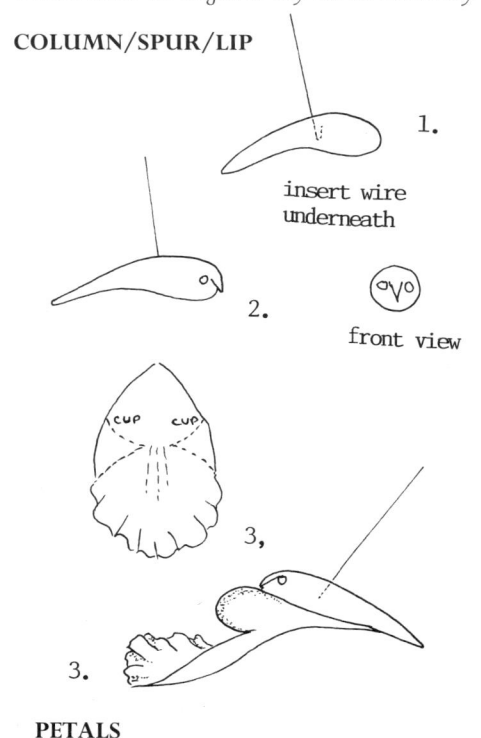

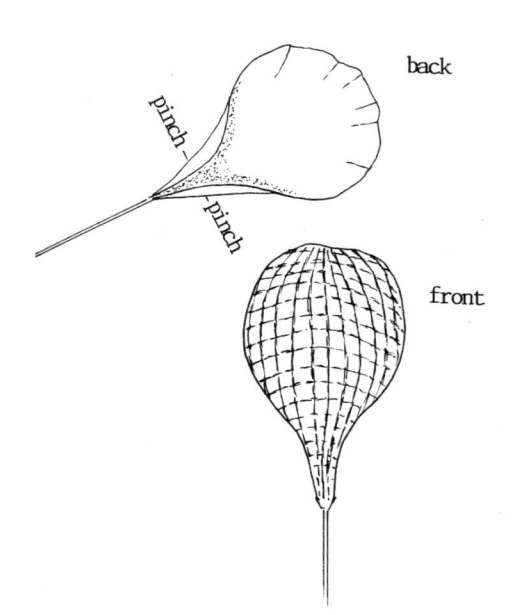

COLUMN/SPUR/LIP

1. Roll a slim carrot-shaped piece of white paste, about ¾ inch (2cm) long.
Make a small hook on a 26 gauge white wire and insert the hook into the paste from below, at an angle, as shown.

2. Snip a tiny 'beak' with fine scissors and mark the 'eyes' with a No. 2 piping nozzle. Curve the tail down and leave to dry.

3. Roll out a piece of white paste quite thinly and cut out a medium rose petal.
Cut away a curved 'vee' on either side, as shown.
Cup the two sides and frill the lower lip quite strongly.
Mark a few lines down the centre of the lip with a narrow veining tool.
Lightly moisten the pointed end of the lip and stick it to the underside of the column, so that hole where the wire entered is hidden.
The two cupped sides are quite close together with the 'beak' in between.
Allow the frilled lip to fall away from the beak, leaving a 'throat'.
Leave to dry, then colour as required. In the Rothschildiana variety, this would be delicate pinky mauve with a little yellow inside and on the tail of the column. The edges of the frilled lip may be deeper mauve with a touch of plum.

PETALS

1. Roll out white paste with a narrow ridge up the centre,.
Cut out two very large rose petals.
Insert a 30 gauge white wire almost to the tip and thin the edges.

2. Vein petals strongly, making sure that the <u>raised</u> veins are on the <u>right</u> side.
Curve the petal back a little and pinch back the lower third so that it looks like a wide stem, as shown.
Leave to dry thoroughly.

3. Make three petals using the medium rose petal cutter.
Vein and shape as above.

4. To colour the petals, first brush a little plum powder over the stems.
Using a flat brush, take deep purple powder colour <u>across</u> the surface of the petals, so that the colour is only picked up on the raised veins and not the spaces in between.
NOTE: The secret of doing this is to make sure that you have very little colour on the brush as any loose grains will fall where they are not wanted and the effect spoilt.

VANDA ORCHID

FLOWER ASSEMBLY

1.

1. Bend the petal wires back very acutely.
Join quarter-width white tape to the wire on the column.

2. Join in the 3 smaller petals at the top with the centre one behind the other two.

3. Join in the two larger petals below, which, because they are pinched back at the base, should fit neatly around and beneath the lip of the trumpet. See drawing below.

4. Tape down all the wires with light green stem tape.

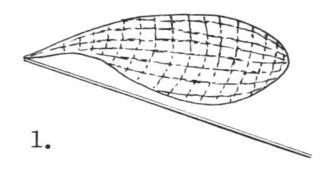

BUDS

1.

1. Vanda orchid buds are quite small and fleshy.
Roll small carrot shapes of white paste and insert white 26 gauge wires which have been taped with light green.
Curve the buds as shown.

2. When dry, brush with light green powder colour.

PLANT ASSEMBLY

1. Tape buds to a 26 gauge wire with light green tape.
The stems are short and curved as shown.

2. Tape in the open orchids as required, adding a 20 or 24 gauge wire for support if necessary.

COUNTRY CUTTERS now make a Vanda Orchid cutter set.

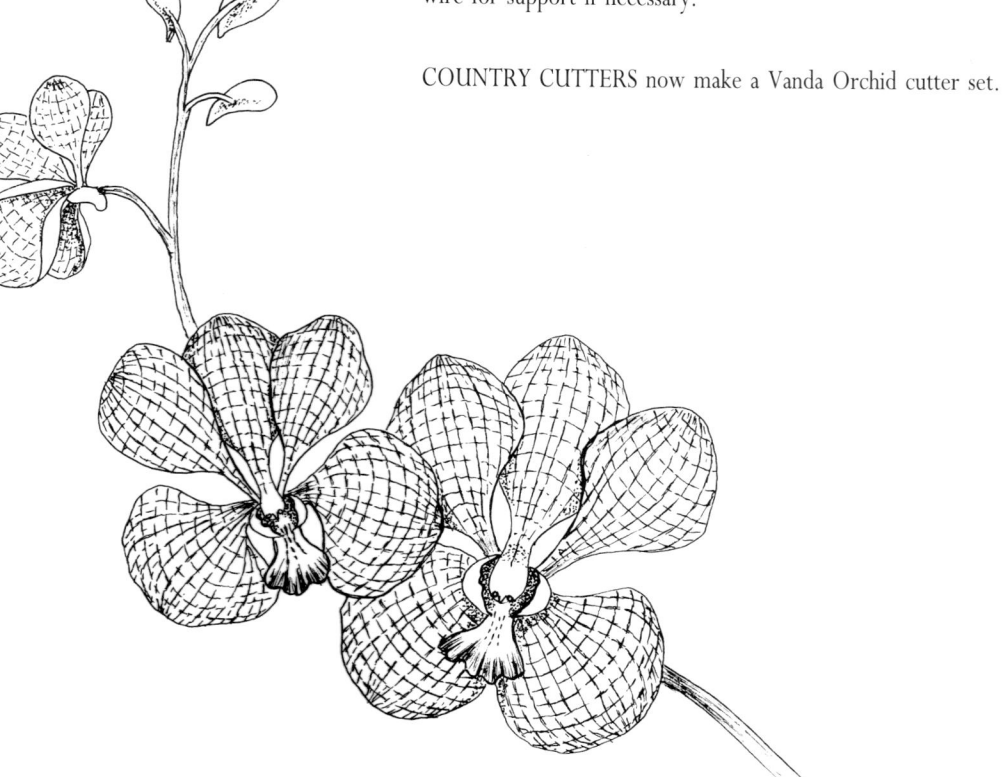

WINTER JASMINE

No colour in the garden to brighten up the day
The snow and frost of winter have frozen it away
Yet hidden in a corner, an unexpected sight -
Yellow winter jasmine sparkles with delight.

Surely the most welcome sight in winter, this pretty little flower makes a promise of brighter days to come. The straight, elegant stems bursting with buds and flowers are so easy to make. Use them in your sprays to accentuate line and shape or in small groups as filler flowers. Either will add a delicate fresh touch.

BUDS

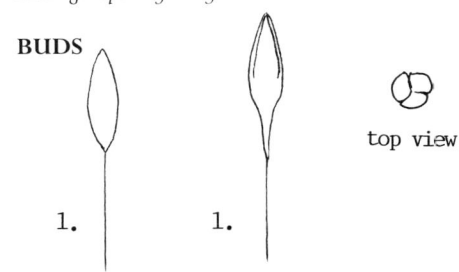

1. Use bright lemon paste. Squires Kitchen daffodil is perfect. Shape a very small piece of paste into a cigar and insert an unhooked 33 gauge green wire, about $3\frac{1}{2}$ inches (9cm) long. Roll one end to make a slim stem, leaving the top part shaped as shown. Mark three lines into the top with a blade for the unopened petals.

2. Make about eight or more buds for each flower stem, from less than $\frac{1}{4}$ inch to just over $\frac{1}{2}$ inch (5mm to 12mm). Leave to dry thoroughly.

CALYX

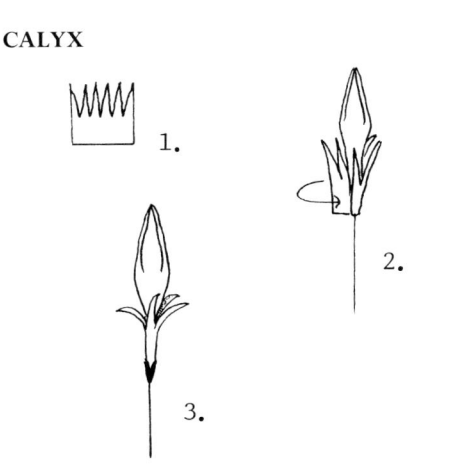

1. Colour paste very light fresh green.
Roll out a small piece very thinly. Using fine, sharp scissors, cut out a tiny fringe. This should be no larger than the drawing, but may be smaller for the tiniest buds.

2. Moisten the lower half of the fringe and lay the stem of the bud in the middle, wrapping the two sides of the fringe around the stem. Roll the stem firmly between the fingers to make it very neat and slim. If necessary, trim away any excess paste at the wire end to reinstate the point.

3. Immediately, before the paste has dried, paint chestnut paste colour, which has been diluted with a drop of water, onto the tips of the sepals. Curl them back a little.
Using slightly stronger chestnut paste colour, paint a two-lobed bud at the very base of the calyx as shown.

OPEN FLOWER

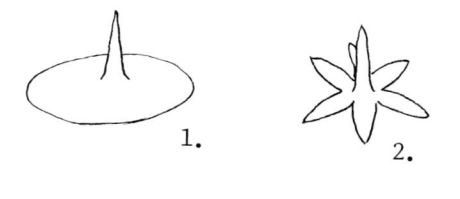

1. Using a very small ball of yellow paste, make a tiny mexican hat with the 'crown' no more than $\frac{1}{4}$ inch (6mm) long, and very slim. Thin the 'brim' as much as possible with the fingers, then roll very finely, making sure that the base of the crown is not too wide or it won't fit into the cutter.

2. Cut out the jasmine flower, using an Orchard six-petalled cutter Size N6.

3. Lay the flower on the firm side of a Cel pad and carefully press the petals with a ball tool. Do not elongate them.
Now slightly widen the petals until they are very fine.

4. Hold the flower in one hand and place the tip of a honiton bobbin in the centre. Do not make a hole, but carefully press each petal against the tool. This will eliminate the thickness at the base of the petals and will open up a very slight indentation which is quite sufficient.

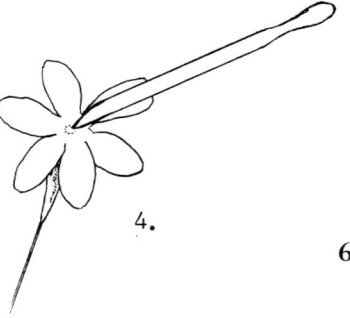

OPEN FLOWER (Continued)

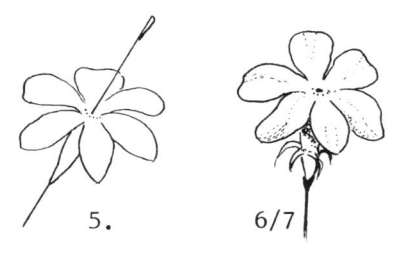

OPEN BUD

DYING FLOWERS

ASSEMBLY

5. Hook a quarter-length light green 30 gauge wire and pull through the flower until only the tip of the hook shows.
This represents the pistil.

6. Re-roll the back of the flower to slim and to secure the wire. Trim stem to $1/2$ inch (12mm) if necessary.
Gently 'move' the petals so that they look very natural.
One or two may be slightly curled or twisted.

7. Complete the calyx and the base bud as before.

1. Make an open flower as above but pull all of the petals forward so that they are not fully open, with three alternate petals inside the remaining three.

2. Complete the calyx and base bud as before.

1. For a dying flower, simply make the open flower, then rest petals on the soft side of a Cel pad and indent all over with a bodkin or small ball tool to 'crumple' the petals.

2. If you want a dead flower, make as above, but 'scrunch' the petals until they look really old. When completely dry, brush the edges of the petals with chestnut paste colour.

3. Complete the calyx as before.

1. Make a very small green bud at the tip of a full-length light green 24 gauge wire. Snip the bud into two as shown. This represents the tiniest unformed buds. Paint base bud with chestnut paste colour.

2. Set out all the buds in size order and bend the wires back immediately below the base buds.

Join quarter-width nile green tape below the green buds and tape down the wire for $1/4$ inch (6mm) only. Tape in the two smallest yellow buds opposite each other, on the left and right of the stem.

3. Tape down for $1/2$ inch (12mm).
Join in two more buds, this time on the front and the back.

4. Tape down for one inch (2.5cm) and add two more buds on the left and right.

5. Continue in this way, adding the buds and then the open buds and the open flowers, gradually increasing the distance on the stem between each pair.
NOTE: It is not necessary to use all the buds before you start using the open buds and open flowers. Create variety by mixing larger buds and flowers as shown.

6. Finish with the dead or dying flowers.

WINTER JASMINE

YEW

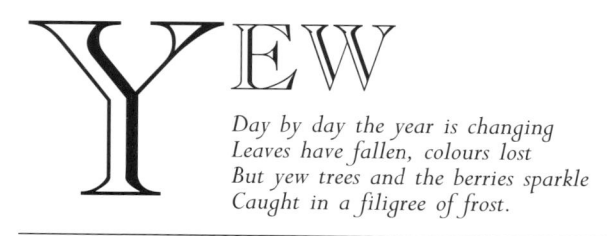

Day by day the year is changing
Leaves have fallen, colours lost
But yew trees and the berries sparkle
Caught in a filigree of frost.

The yew, with its many tiny leaves is not an obvious item to be included in a sugarcraft book, but I have chosen it because it is unusual and, anyway, you only need a very small 'token' spray to enhance your winter arrangement. This is the very last entry in the Four Seasons books, so how could I leave you without one final challenge.

LEAVES (PASTE METHOD)

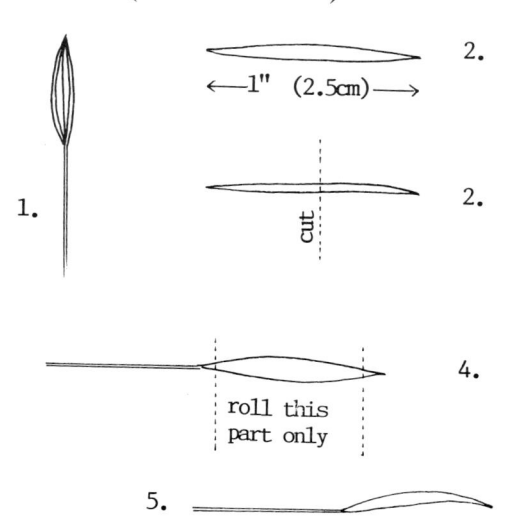

1. Colour paste mid/dark green. Make a long, slim bud on a hooked, half-length 28 gauge dark green wire. Mark bud with a sharp blade to look like unopened leaves.

2. Cut 45 to 50 pieces of fine uncovered rose wire, about 2 inches (5cm) long. Roll a tiny ball of paste into a very thin sausage, one inch (2.5cm) long with a point at both ends. Cut in half.

3. Take one piece and 'twizzle' the cut end to re-establish the shape as the cut of the blade will have squashed it. Insert the wire, pushing it up as far as possible without breaking through the tip. Roll again to re-shape as shown.

4. Lay leaf on a board and flatten with a small rolling tool between the two ends. Do not roll over the points as this will spoil the shape.

5. Curve leaves slightly and leave to dry.

LEAVES (TAPE METHOD)

1. Cut a one yard (1 metre) piece of dark green stem tape and shred it into four lengths. Twist each quarter-width into 'fronds', stretching as you go so that the final frond is as long as it can be.

2. Bind each length around a medium rolling pin and roll firmly on a board to flatten the twisted tape.

3. Measure lengths for the needles as required: several at 1½ inches (4cm), and then longer, up to 2 inches (5cm), and BREAK off. Do NOT cut. This will ensure that the tips will be pointed and fine.

4. Fold each length in half to make pairs of needles.

BERRIES

1. Colour paste deep rose. Make a pea-sized oval ball. Hollow out one end and insert a 30 gauge dark green wire, with a very small ski-stick (see glossary). Pull well down inside.

2. Drop a very small black ball into the hole, for the seed and leave to dry.

3. Drip some confectioners glaze into the hole so that only the black seed is glazed, not the outside of the berry.

YEW

ASSEMBLY

1. Tape the needles below the bud, as shown. Do not let the silver rose wires show.
If using tape needles, catch in only the extreme lower folded end of each pair.

2. Tape in the berries as required, close to the stem.

FLOWER PASTE

There are many new ready-made flower pastes on the market. I have tried the paste made by Squires Kitchen and by Diamond Paste & Mould Company, both of which I can thoroughly recommend.

For those people who prefer to make their own paste, may I refer you to the recipes in The Four Seasons books - Spring and Summer.